LIBERAL JUDAISM AT HOME

LIBERAL JUDAISM AT HOME

The Practices of Modern Reform Judaism

Morrison David Bial
Rabbi, Temple Sinai

UNION OF AMERICAN HEBREW CONGREGATIONS

Preface

The purpose of this book is to present the practices of Liberal Judaism in relationship to the accepted norms of traditional Judaism. No one until now has attempted to juxtapose traditional practice to Liberal practice and to explain how they differ. This book will try to make explicit to the layman that which has too often been vague and unstated.

Despite the wide spectrum of ritual and its observance, there is a discernible pattern in Reform practice. Most is based on traditional Jewish ritual and custom. Where it has links with what has gone before, this book presents a brief account of the custom or law from which it grew and a presentation of how it is observed in Liberal Judaism. At times, a reason for the change can be adduced, and this is offered—though it must be understood that not everyone will agree with the reasons offered. The processes of history and change are not always logical.

Not all Reform Jewish practice is based on traditional Judaism. Some practices have been borrowed from the cultures and religions that surround the Jewish community. So confirmation and consecration are presented along with their background and evolution.

There are some Orthodox rituals which have disappeared entirely among most Liberal Jews, and some of these are included in this presentation for the picture they provide of the variety and depth of traditional Jewish practice.

It is my hope that this presentation will have value to the Liberal Jew who is seeking a positive understanding of the rituals and practices of Liberal Judaism as he and his family observe them.

My sincere thanks to colleagues and friends who assisted me: Rabbi Hillel Gamoran for his careful reading and sage advice; Rabbi William Horn and Rabbi Louis Sigel who helped with many a *sheilah* on tradition; Rabbi William Braude and Rabbi Solomon Freehof for answering a number of questions and for the whole corpus of their work in this field; and to the members of my congregation who provided the incentive and the encouragement for this book, my profound gratitude to them all.

MORRISON DAVID BIAL

Summit, N.J., 1967, 1971
5727, 5731

Credits

All photos, except page 150, courtesy of UAHC Synagogue Architectural Library.

Page ii, Ark of polished Israeli marble. Sculpture, by Jan Peter Stern, in stainless steel, incorporates Ner Tamid in symbolic representation of the Tree of Life with apex suggesting menorah. Percival Goodman, F.I.I.A., architect. Stained glass, by Robert Pinart. Congregation Shaaray Zedek, Southfield, Michigan. **P. 2,** Sephardic synagogue in Old Jerusalem, by David Zak. Photo, New York Times. **P. 10,** Circumcision plate. Galicia, early nineteenth century. **P. 16,** "The Blessing," Walter Midener. **P. 24,** "The Lesson," Moissaye Marans. Temple Emanu-El, Houston, Texas. **P. 27,** Detail of mosaic, "Prayer, Study, and Assembly," by Joseph Young. Temple Emanu-El, Beverly Hills, California. **P. 30,** "Teacher," limestone, Shay Rieger. **P. 36,** "Rejoicing of the Law," bronze, Luise Kaish. Congregation B'rith Kodesh, Rochester, New York. Photo, Sculpture Center. **P. 42,** Chupah, Efrem Weitzman. Rodeph Sholom, New York City. **P. 47,** Golden bridal ring, given by bridegroom. Italy, sixteenth century. Photo, the Jewish Museum of the Hebrew Union College. **P. 56,** Detail of sculpture, by Sidney Simon, for Temple Beth Abraham, Tarrytown, New York. Photo, Paul Cordes. **P. 62,** Sanctuary—Ark doors, designed by A. Raymond Katz, executed by Don Ben Aaron. Perpetual Light, bronze, designed by A. Raymond Katz, executed by Beacon Artisans. Stained-glass windows, designed by Rodney Winfield of Emil Frei, Inc. Architects, Walter H. Sobel and J. Stewart Stein. Oak Park Temple, Oak Park, Illinois. Photo, Bill Engdahl, Hedrich-Blessing, Chicago, Illinois. **P. 72,** Mezuzah, brass, by Victor Ries. **P. 80,** "Pomegranate," Torah breastplate and crowns, by William B. Meyers. Photo, John Geraci. **P. 86,** "The Doors of the Thirty-Six," sterling silver, by Ilya Schor. Temple Beth El, Great Neck, New York. **P. 92,** Eternal Light, by Helen Burke.

P. 101, Model for "Yea though I walk in the Valley of the Shadow of Death," by Alice A. Richheimer. Photo, W. B. Nickerson, Evanston, Illinois. **P. 104,** Memorial to the victims of the Holocaust, Greenwood Cemetery, Atlanta, Georgia. Benjamin Hirsch, A.I.A. Photo, William A. Barnes. **P. 116,** Omer calendar, silver frame and hand painted parchment, by Maurice Mayer. **P. 122,** Synagogue kiddish cup, UAHC, designed and executed by William B. Meyers. **P. 138,** "The Law," by Milton Horn. **P. 145,** Tzedakah box, silver and bronze, by Maxwell Chayat. **P. 150,** Sukah, designed by John Friedler. Temple Sinai, Summit, New Jersey. **P. 155,** Etrog box, by Ludwig Wolpert. Photo, Darmstaedter. **P. 158,** "Sunray," menorah by William B. Meyers. Photo, John Geraci. **P. 161,** Stained-glass window, by Leon Gordon Miller. Temple on the Heights, Cleveland, Ohio. Rebman Photo Service. **P. 164,** Megillah cover, by Rolando Poggianti, Florence, Italy. **P. 167,** Woodcut, by Ilya Schor, from a megillah issued by the Commission on Synagogue Activities of the UAHC. **P. 168,** Seder plate, pewter, Germany, 1776. The Jewish Museum of the Hebrew Union College, Cincinnati, Ohio. **P. 178,** "Shavuoth," sculptural decoration, by George Aarons, for the Hillel Foundation building, University of Connecticut, Storrs, Connecticut. **P. 181,** Stained-glass window, "Ruth and Naomi," by Ellen Simon. **P. 182,** Wailing Wall, terra cotta, by Berta Margoulies. Photo, Oliver Baker, New York. **P. 186,** Havdalah set, by Ludwig Wolpert. Photo, Darmstaedter. **P. 204,** Window grills, by Victor Ries. Jewish Community Center, San Raphael, California. Photo, Ruth Bernhard, San Francisco.

Editor's Introduction

The synagog is the central institution of Judaism today although it never was prior to the modern period. The home occupied that position of prominence and served as the primary preserver of Jewish values and practices. Morrison Bial emphasizes the traditions that a Jew can practice without dependence on the synagog as a ceremonial institution.

Rabbi Bial's emphasis on personal practice does not disparage the synagog in any way; rather it encourages the Jew to realize the importance, if not the urgency, of returning Judaism to the home where it rightfully belongs. The Jewish heritage is severely bereft when removed from either synagog or home.

It is in the home, however, that the young Jew first sees the beauty of Judaism, experiencing his Jewish tradition sensuously and emotionally as well as intellectually. It is the atmosphere of the home that determines the firmness of Jewish loyalty just as the soil and sunlight determine the healthiness of a plant.

The Jew worships and studies and socializes in the synagog which has basic and important functions commonly experienced in prescribed segments of time. But he lives in his home and, if the home is filled with the ambiance, the "flavor," of Judaism, then he lives naturally and genuinely as a Jew.

The author endeavors to show his readers the ways that they can create this ambiance in their homes, this sense of Jewishness in their personal lives so that an unfair and unrealistic onus does not continue to fall upon the synagog for the deepening of Jewish life.

Commenting on the verse from Nehemiah 10, "Set up ordinances for yourselves," the great poet Chayim Nachman Bialik wrote: "So did your ancestors begin to rebuild their homes." Thus our homes can be built Jewishly if the customs and ceremonies of Judaism are practiced as a vital part of our lives. May this book guide the reader toward the Judaization of his life and the needed personalization of Judaism.

Jack D. Spiro

Contents

LIBERAL JUDAISM AT HOME

The Criteria of Reform Jewish Practice

The purpose of this book is to help Liberal Jews determine what is customary Reform practice, especially as it affects them personally. We will not deal with synagogal practice except in passing, as rabbis and ritual committees have determined the procedure of the temples. Though members have the right to question and to suggest changes, each congregation must set its own standards and norms for its services and for those who participate in them.

However, the synagog does not establish standards for members' individual and private lives. The Liberal Jew's personal practices, within his home and in his private life, these are the subject of this book. From the first, Liberal Jews have refused to be bound by any code of Jewish practice. At the earliest conferences of Liberal rabbis, in the 1840's, decisions were made on such basic items as the day of the Sabbath, the use of Hebrew, circumcision, wedding procedures, etc. In some instances the rabbis made decisions and their congregations refused to heed them on their return home. The congregations insisted on being autonomous, and individual Liberal Jews felt that any code would be dictation.

3

This is my God and I will glorify Him

Today, too, the majority of the Liberal Jews feel that any establishment of standards would lead to regimentation and would deny individual responsibility, which has always been the touchstone of the Liberal Jew. Also, any such code, no matter how vaguely worded, would set limits to individual decision, and might well harden into rigid lines. Our movement is called Reform Judaism, and not "Reformed," as it is sometimes mislabeled.

Yet with the proliferation of Liberal congregations and the addition to our ranks of hundreds of thousands of Jews, there are many who seek counsel and guides to their private observance. Attempts have been made to establish such guides. These have demonstrated arduous thought and great devotion. There are other smaller guides which are the relatively brief compendia of the decisions of the ritual committee of a certain congregation or the labors of one particular rabbi. None of these guides has attempted to show the traditional background of the practices they discuss, how the traditional customs arose, and how Liberal Jews have chosen among them and how Liberal Jews practice them today.

This is not a simple task. Unlike congregational practices, it is almost impossible to establish what are the usual practices of the varying individuals who call themselves Reform Jews. The Union of American Hebrew Congregations often conducts surveys of congregational procedures. These are printed and distributed, so that it is possible to discover how many temples hold Bar or Bat Mitzvah, the age of confirmands, the percentage of rabbis who wear an *atarah* at services, etc. One can also learn the direction congregations are tending in their ritual observances by comparing the figures with those of past decades.

However, attempts to chart the usual practices of Reform individuals have been piecemeal and inconclusive. We do not know the number or percentage who light candles on Sabbath eves or keep *kosher* homes, or who smoke on Yom Kippur. Even if such figures existed, would they have any validity to help establish what correct, thoughtful, efficacious Reform Jewish practice should be?

Orthodox Practice

Establishing the legal basis of Orthodox Jewish religious practice is not difficult. In the sixteenth century, Joseph Karo, living in Safed in Turkish Palestine, compiled the four thick volumes of the *Shulchan Aruch,* the "Prepared Table." In these books he codified all of Jewish law as it pertained to the individual, the community and to the congregation. Anyone who could read Hebrew could determine Jewish law on any usual situation. Although there were prior attempts to produce a code of Jewish law that would be intelligible to the average informed Jew, notably those of Maimonides and of Asher ben Joseph, these earlier works were beyond the comprehension of any but talmudic scholars.

Karo's work soon became the standard guide to traditional Jewish life. As Karo was a Sephardic Jew, the book reflected his upbringing. Moses Isserles, a Polish rabbi, added a commentary to the "Prepared Table" which he called *Mapah,* the "Tablecloth." It supplies those rules and customs which were peculiar to Ashkenazic Jews. With Karo's and Isserles' work before him, the *baal ha-bayit,* Mr. Average Jew, was prepared to face any usual manifestation of life, from arising in the morning through his business day, his religious life, his matrimonial life, the duties of a husband to a wife and vice versa, and much more. The Table was truly Prepared.

But even this detailed compendium of Jewish law was not sufficient to establish the whole face of Jewish tradition. In every part of the world where Jews lived, there had arisen practices which were indigenous to that area alone, and which soon hardened into *minhag,* custom, which had all the force of law. These customs varied from the most simple and picturesque—in Germany the infant's swaddling band was later embroidered and became a Torah wrapper—to the most superstitious; in some areas a glass of water was placed in the room with a corpse so that the soul could wash itself. Some customs held for only a small district. Others became an integral part of the lives of millions. So Jews in some towns celebrated a local Purim to commemorate a deliverance from a tyrant. On the other hand, millions of Jews considered whistling to be a method of provoking or calling the evil spirits and frowned upon it as dangerous, though there is nothing in Jewish law to substantiate this belief.

Sometimes a rabbi's decision continued in force hundreds of years after his death—Sephardic Jews may eat rice on Pesach; Ashkenazic Jews may not. Sometimes a borrowing from non-Jewish neighbors became so Jewish a custom that after centuries of use even the gentiles considered that which was once borrowed from them a necessity of Jewish religious life—the braided *chalah* for Sabbath, which is a borrowing of the *barches brot* of early, pagan Germany.

Trying to trace each of these additions and accretions, to classify them as those laws and customs which are derived from the Bible or the Talmud, as rabbinic *takanot*, emendations, or as borrowings from the Gentiles, or as superstitions, would provide a task for a series of doctoral dissertations. Yet we must be aware of this mixed background of traditional Jewish practice for it may illuminate our goal, the study of Reform Jewish practice. If at times it transpires that Reform practice may seem arbitrary, or derived from customs of our non-Jewish neighbors, or from the recent decisions of Liberal rabbis, knowing the course of Orthodox development will help make it clear to us that Liberal Judaism has arisen in a manner not entirely dissimilar.

It is true that at times Reform teaching contravenes biblical or talmudic ordinance. Liberal Judaism, though respecting the historical importance of the Talmud and always eager to learn from its wisdom, does not feel bound by its legislation. The teachings of the Bible are more important to Liberal Jews; the Orthodox hold the Talmud to be equally sacred and equally binding. But even those who were most scrupulous in upholding tradition have felt free to reinterpret and even to change biblical pronouncements. A most important legal contrivance of the eminent Hillel, in the first century B.C.E., is called the *prosbul*. It is unquestionably a contravention of a scriptural law concerning borrowing which was causing hardship to the farmer. He resolved the difficulty through the *prosbul* which made it possible for the poor farmer to borrow at the approach of the sabbatical year. Hillel was a strict observer of traditional law, and yet a rebel and reformer.

So Liberal Judaism's manner of observing our religion is based on the varying elements that have shaped all of Jewish life. A significant portion of our observance is related to scriptural teaching. There is much derived from the Talmud and from the *takanot* and responsa of two millennia of rabbis. Some of our practices are traceable to conscious decisions of early reformers, rabbis and laymen, made in conferences or at synagog meetings. Others seem simply to have grown by themselves.

It is clear, however, that the principle of change and development which is basic to Reform Judaism is not an innovation. On the contrary, for centuries in the past Judaism evolved new forms and new ways to meet new circumstances.

Conservative Philosophy and Practice

Conservative Judaism occupies a middle ground between Orthodoxy and Reform. In theology it is closer to Reform; in practice it is often closer to tradition. The gradations of observance vary so greatly among Conservative adherents that it would be impossible for us to use them as a touchstone in our description of the ways of either Orthodox or Reform Jews. Some Conservative Jews endeavor to fulfill just about all the usual Orthodox practices, with only minor differences. Other Conservative Jews might well be members of Liberal congregations, as they are untraditional in thought and in habit. Thus it is not always easy to contrast Reform with Conservative practice. Furthermore, Conservative Judaism developed after Reform and so we need not deal with it in tracing developments in Reform. For these reasons, Conservatism will not figure largely in this work.

Our contrast will be between the usual traditional with the usual Liberal way.

Unlike some other works which have tried to provide a code of practice for Reform Jews, this book will not try to establish norms or definite procedures. The history and the spirit of Liberal Judaism are both against any setting of such criteria. The Liberal Jew has, by his own tradition, the duty to study what has been customary Jewish observance, consider the reasoning that established these traditions, and then survey usual Reform practice. With this knowledge he must establish his own personal reaction and way of Jewish life. To serve as a tool for the seeking, thinking Liberal Jew is the intent of this work.

The Final Criterion

The major difficulty with the criterion we have mentioned, his own sense of spiritual values, arrived at by diligent study of tradition—is that it obviously sets each Liberal Jew as his own judge of what he will or will not do.

To the traditional Jew this is nothing less than a severe transgression of *halachah,* the law. It is God who established the Torah and its *mitzvot,* commandments. Anyone who would dare set any *mitzvah,* commandment, aside is one who would cut at the roots of the God-given religion.

Then what can the Liberal Jew use as his final criterion, to help his knowledge of tradition and his understanding of

Liberal Judaism in the task of deciding just where he fits in the infinite spectrum of Jewish observance? The answer must be a sense of *kedushah,* of holiness, of that which will help him sanctify his life, to make it truly meaningful. By this must he live, and it will help give his life that inner meaning by which we seek fulfillment.

A glossary defining all Hebrew, Aramaic and Yiddish terms begins on page 187.

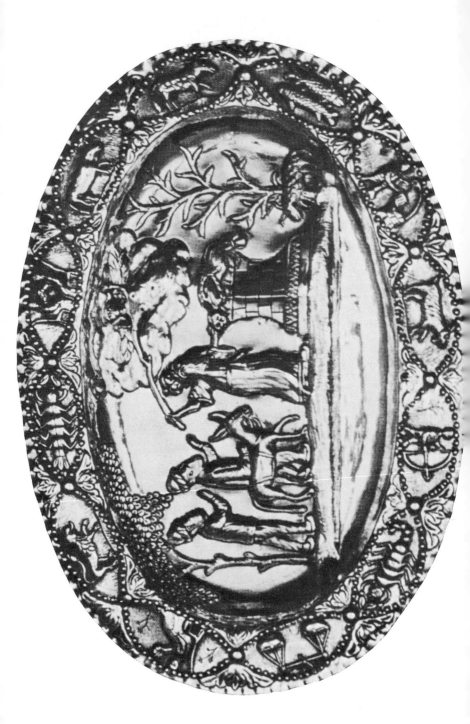

Lay not your hand on the lad

Birth

Lo, children are a heritage of the Lord;
The fruit of the womb is a reward.

PSALMS 127:3

Birth is more than just the beginning of life: it is a blessing and a responsibility, a fulfillment and a joy. God's first command to man is, "Be fruitful and multiply!" In Judaism children have always been considered a gift and a duty. Though a man might wish to dedicate himself to the great Jewish ideals of study and prayer, he is enjoined to marry and father children. The rabbis discussed this in great detail. The stricter sages demanded that his union produce two sons before a man could feel that he had done his duty. Hillel, always the compassionate, said that a son and a daughter would suffice. Even he when confronted by a man with six daughters would have to sigh and say the job was incomplete. At least one son was needed.

Liberal Judaism, with its insistence on the equality of the sexes, would no longer hold that male issue is indispensable. Our Orthodox brethren consider a boy of greater importance as he is the parents' *kaddish*. Only a son can recite the great affirmation of faith after their death, or so say the Orthodox. A girl, devoted and devout as she might be, is not counted in a *minyan*, the quorum of ten men needed for community prayer, and so Orthodox parents must hope for a male. Not

11

that girls are unwanted. Given his *kaddish* (the first-born male is actually referred to by the name of the prayer he will someday recite), a man would dandle his daughters with delight. But the Orthodox always bear in mind the words of the Talmud: "The birth of a male child brings peace into the world" (*Nidah* 31b).

Liberal Jews do not place importance on the sex of their progeny for any religious reason, for a daughter may recite the *Kaddish* just as well as a son, and women are counted in a *minyan*.

Birth Control

Orthodoxy is intent on many births, and contraception is not readily countenanced. Although Professor Lauterbach spent pages (CCAR *Journal,* Vol. 37, pp. 369-384) trying to prove that birth control is not really contrary to Jewish tradition, most rabbis would agree that the weight of evidence is against him. Yet when a woman's health is in danger or outside exigency demanding, even Orthodox rabbis condone contraceptives. However, only the woman may wear a device, for the man's doing so would be too akin to the story of Onan (Genesis 38:9).

Liberal Judaism considers the bearing of children as natural fulfillment, yet recognizes the right of children to be born into homes where they are desired and can be provided for. Therefore any medically accepted contraceptive is approved as long as it does not prohibit later conception and birth.

Abortion

Judaism is concerned with the sanctity of life and its preservation. Therefore, the very idea of abortion is approached with caution. In traditional Judaism only when the woman's life is endangered is abortion allowed. If medical opinion states that she will die or is in grave danger because of her pregnancy, no Orthodox rabbi or physician would hesitate. If the danger is psychical, a threat to her mental well-being, the traditional conservatism of Orthodoxy would be firmly opposed to abortion except in the most pressing exigency—despite the fact that the foetus is not considered to be a living soul until it is born, or, more technically speaking, mostly born. When the head and a shoulder emerge into the world, then the infant is born and is considered to be dowered with a soul. Until then, it is considered part of the mother. Indeed, if the foetus is threatening the mother's health, the Talmud considers the foetus in the same category as one who brandishes a sword, and it must be destroyed.

However, if the mother's health and mental state are unexceptional, rare would be the traditional Jew who would even consider an abortion.

This contrasts with the usual Reform thought which would allow a woman to have control of her own body as it does with her own destiny. A woman with an unwanted pregnancy, especially when she is underage, or the pregnancy is the result of rape or incest or seduction, would be counselled to have it terminated. Any admonition that she should "pay" for her sinning would be unconscionable in Liberal Judaism. And for that matter, if a married woman has had a number of children and finds herself pregnant with an unwanted child, after serious discussion most Liberal rabbis would agree with its termination.

Nonetheless, abortion is always a major step and never to be entered into lightly.

Sterilization

As the medical practice of sterilization is recent it has little precedent in the Jewish tradition. The idea of any person's being sterilized would be repugnant to Jewish traditionalists. Perhaps, when there is real physical danger to a woman if she were to become pregnant, the Orthodox might give their reluctant permission. Probably they would not give this permission to her husband, even though a vasectomy is easier than the similar operation on his wife, because of the biblical condemnation of the sin of Onan. Also, there is always a chance that the wife may die or he may divorce her, and he would be left unable to procreate and thus be unable fully to enter into a new marriage.

Liberal Judaism maintains that an individual has control of his own body. Therefore, if a couple who have had some children decide for cogent reason that they wish to have no more, they may decide on one of them being sterilized. As a vasectomy is usually easier, the Liberal rabbinate would probably not insist on a woman's undergoing the operation. But the man must be aware of the possibility that he might be in a position to remarry and not be able to father a new family.

An additional situation to consider is where one or the other partner has genetic problems in his background and might want sterilization to preclude continuing such a danger to a new generation. Liberal Judaism would probably accept such a decision. Orthodoxy would probably say that unless the genetic condition is so absolutely certain that a monster would be born, the couple should have faith and trust that all will be well.

So too, when a defective child is born and it matures, Liberal Judaism might advocate its being sterilized, especially as it might well be taken advantage of. Orthodoxy would hesitate even here.

Birth

Preparation for birth is not only physical. When the baby arrives the family rabbi should be informed. He will want to visit the mother at the hospital. On beholding their child for the first time, parents may want to say the *Shehecheyanu* prayer, the blessing said at all happy times. *Baruch Atah Adonai, Elohenu Melech ha-olam, shehecheyanu, vekiyemanu, vehigianu lazeman hazeh.* "Blessed art thou, O Lord our God, King of the universe, who hast kept us in life, sustained us, and brought us to this time."

There are many old customs and superstitions that used to surround the time of birth. Considering its grave danger until quite recently, this is not surprising. Much of the danger in the days before knowledge of germs was attributed to evil spirits, especially Lilith, Adam's demon wife. The birth bed was hung with amulets. Sometimes a key, especially the key to the synagog, was placed under the pillow of the woman in labor. Sometimes an axe was placed under the bed or a knife under the pillow, to cut the labor pains. All these are only superstitions that have no place in modern Judaism.

Milah

When the newcomer is a male, arrangements for his circumcision should be made. Many hospitals today circumcise all male infants, regardless of religion. It is a hygienic measure, vindicating the prescience of our ancestors. Informed that the hospital will take care of this matter, some parents assume that this is all that is necessary, and forget the religious ceremony that should accompany the operation. This is unfortunate, and deprives the family and the infant of a meaningful and joyful ceremony. *Milah,* circumcision, as a religious rite is of fundamental importance to the religious existence of Israel. The usual word we use for the ceremony is *berit,* which means covenant, or *berit milah,* the covenant of circumcision. So significant is *berit milah* that Baruch Spinoza declared: "Such great importance do I attach to the sign of the Covenant, that I am persuaded it is sufficient by itself to maintain the exist-

The Lord bless you and keep you

ence of the nation forever" (*Theologico-Political Treatise,* Chapter 3).

If a *mohel,* a traditional circumciser, is to perform the operation—in many larger communities such practitioners of an ancient craft are attached to the hospital staff—the rabbi is not necessary at the ceremony as the *mohel* performs both the surgery and the religious ritual. It is interesting to note that when the present Prince of Wales was born, his parents requested of the Chief Rabbi the name of a *mohel,* who performed the operation on the heir to the throne. Needless to say, the surgery sans any rite did not turn the prince into a Jew.

If a surgeon is to perform the operation, the rabbi will assume the religious duty. Whether the service is conducted by a *mohel* or a rabbi, it is the father's role to recite the traditional prayer in presenting his son for circumcision.

Usually this is a family celebration, and some hospitals provide proper quarters so that members of the family may attend. Where the hospital does not provide such space, the father and grandfathers and the rabbi should attend, to present the child.

The traditional *minyan,* quorum of ten men, is not needed in Liberal Judaism. The Orthodox ask for the *minyan* as the *berit* used to be performed in the synagog, after morning worship. Nor is the traditional feast following the ceremony more than a pleasant custom. If the father is unavoidably away at the time of the *berit,* it should not be deferred. An uncle or grandfather should act in his stead, reciting the benediction, changing only the phrase "my son" to "my nephew" or "my grandson."

There is a Jewish form of godparent, the *sandek,* who played an important role at the *berit.* This word is of Greek origin and indicates the man who held the child on his knees during the operation. Today the *sandek's* role is a position of honor with little to do. The wife of the *sandek* presents the child to the *sandek.* To provide even more honors for friends and relations, the additional roles of *kvatter* and *kvatterin,* from the German *Gevatter,* were introduced. Liberal Jews may so designate friends if they wish to, but there is no real significance to their roles today.

There are a few hospitals which prohibit a rabbi's attendance if a surgeon rather than a *mohel* operates. This is a rule highly to be condemned. In such instances, the child should be brought home before the eighth day and the ceremony performed there.

It is true that if for medical or other overriding reason the child was not circumcised—or circumcised without the ceremony—he is still a Jew, yet circumcision must not be taken lightly.

The Proper Day

Because many crowded hospitals demand that mother and child leave before a full week has passed, some parents may ask to have the circumcision done before the eighth day. Tradition speaks loudly against this idea. If a baby's health demands, the rite can be postponed until he is strong enough. However, anticipating the eighth day is not countenanced in Judaism. Professor Israel Bettan, in his responsum (CCAR *Journal,* 1954) protested this hurrying of a religious rite for mere expediency. If the mother and child leave the hospital before the eighth day, arrangements should be made for the circumcision in the house or at the hospital on an "outpatient" basis.

Physicians have often stated that the eighth day seems the best time. The infant is usually strong enough and yet young enough that the nervous system is still relatively unformed, so there is relatively little shock. *Milah* is performed on the eighth day though it be the Sabbath or even a festival or High Holy Day. When a *berit* is deferred, it may not take place on these days.

A legally adopted son is subject to *milah*. If he has already been circumcised, he should not be subjected to the shedding of a single drop of blood, as is Orthodox custom. Rather should he be blessed and given a Hebrew name by the rabbi. A son born of a non-Jewish father (if the father has been converted to Judaism, he and his son are both Jews in every sense of the word) is presented for the *berit* by a relative of the mother or by the rabbi.

A boy born out of wedlock is considered completely "legitimate" in Reform Judaism and may hold any temple office or become a rabbi or cantor, or, if a girl, marry a rabbi or cantor, when old enough. A boy born out of wedlock is presented for circumcision by a relative of the mother or by the rabbi.

Mamzerut

According to Orthodoxy a *mamzer,* bastard, is not the offspring of an unmarried mother. An illegitimate child is no different from any other Jew. Even in Orthodoxy such a child may grow to be a pillar of the community. A *mamzer* is a child born to an impossible union, to a man and a woman married to another man. Their child is a *mamzer,* and can never enter into the congregation and so can only mate with another *mamzer.* The Orthodox restrictions on *mamzerut,* traditional illegitimacy, were safeguards to protect the institution of marriage, but Liberal Jews would never go so far as to attempt to cut a child off from the body of Judaism. If a married woman bears another man's child we are dismayed, but it would be invidious to label the child and distort its life.

The Chair of Elijah

Although the Orthodox differ as to the legitimacy of clamps or other mechanical devices at a circumcision, Liberal Judaism allows any proper surgical procedure. The use of wine at a *berit* is an old custom and is still used by Liberal Jews.

Among the older customs of *milah* are the *Kise Eliyahu*, the Chair of Elijah. Elijah accused the Israelites of forsaking the covenant (I Kings 19:10–14). So the sages said that God ordained that Elijah be present at every *berit*, so that he might see for himself that Jews still are faithful. This custom is not usual among Liberal Jews.

Blessing and Naming

In most Liberal congregations all babies, boys as well as girls, are blessed. In some temples the parents bring the child as soon as all three are ready to travel and the rabbi asks God's blessings on the infant before the open ark. Most congregations ask the parents to be present at the first service following the birth which the mother is able to attend, preferably during the first month. A lovely certificate, published by the Union of American Hebrew Congregations, is presented by the congregation to the happy parents. If the public blessing must be deferred, the rabbi will, on his visit to the home, bless and name the child, and the public blessing may follow.

The certificate has room for Hebrew as well as English names. If the parents do not have any Hebrew names in mind, the rabbi will probably find suitable equivalents.

Often a child is named for a deceased relative. This is not as ancient a custom as some imagine. Certainly it is not biblical or talmudic in origin. Central European Jews considered it a form of honoring the deceased. Traditional practice, especially Ashkenazic (Central European), was not to name a child for any living person. As this was probably based on superstitious fear, some Reform Jews pay no attention to it. Certainly there is no valid reason except the force of tradition and such domestic difficulties as may ensue.

Jews have not always used biblical names, even though

there is certainly a return to this noble practice. There are a number of rabbis in the Talmud with Greek names, such as Pappas and Julianus. The Talmud states, "The majority of Jews in exile had names like Gentiles" (*Gittin* 11b). However, certain names closely connected with other faiths ought to be discarded. It might be well to consider the meaning of a name before choosing it. Avoid one like Christopher, Dolores, or Natalie, names with a basic meaning in another religion. "A man's name is the essence of his being" (*Sefer Ziyuni,* Menachem ben Meier of Speyer, Cremona, p. 26). Adopted children should be named at the temple within a month of their adoption whether there is circumcision or not, and given a Hebrew name.

The name of the person memorialized may be changed to fit the infant, who may be of the opposite sex. There is no reason why a son should not be named for a deceased grandmother, or a daughter for her grandfather. Any qualms are the heritages of an old superstition: the soul of the grandfather might be tempted by his name reappearing on earth to descend and enter the body of the infant and thus be tricked into living the life of a woman.

The fear of naming a child after another who died young, or a person who met an untimely end, too, is only a superstition. The rabbis suggested adding another name for reassurance.

Pidyon ha-Ben

An exceedingly ancient rite that is all but forgotten by Liberal Jews is *pidyon ha-ben,* the redemption of the first-born son. According to the Bible, the first-born son of the mother belongs to the priest, unless a girl or a stillbirth has preceded him. Rather than turn him over to the priest, the traditional Jew redeems him with five silver pieces. If either parent is a descendant of a Kohen (temple priest) or a Levite (temple attendant), they are exempt from the duty.

The day of the ceremony is the thirty-first after birth, unless it falls on a Sabbath or holy day, when it is postponed to the day following. Usually the five pieces of silver (silver dollars are impressive but five dollars in any form will do) are donated to a charity, though the "priest" who accepts them has a right to keep them. Usually a small party would follow. Liberal Jews do not often observe this rite.

Other Customs

One of the loveliest of ancient customs was the planting of a tree to mark a birth. For a son a cedar was planted; for a daughter, a pine or cypress. Subsequently, the bridal chamber was built from the wood of the two trees the parents had planted. Paying to have a tree planted in the UAHC forest in Israel is an easy and beneficial way of observing this old custom, though using its wood at the marriage might be difficult to arrange.

A strange old custom known to most of us only by hearsay is the cutting of an infant's hair for the first time as a ceremony. A festive meal was prepared, during which each guest would be invited to cut a few hairs, careful lest the *peot* or sidelocks be infringed upon. This tonsorial exercise was usually on Lag Ba-Omer, the one day an Orthodox Jew would allow his hair to be cut between Pesach and Shavuot.

The Childless

According to traditional law a childless couple must seek a divorce after ten years of connubial life, so that each may have another opportunity of becoming a parent with a new and perhaps more fertile mate. The rabbis recognized this to be harsh at times, but the requirement to bear children was considered all important. Liberal Judaism suggests that a childless couple do all in their power to have children (test-tube children are not considered illegitimate), and then adopt at least one child, if it can be arranged. They may, where state law permits, adopt a non-Jewish child with the understanding that it be reared as a Jew. Such a child need not be converted for it is considered a Jew as though from birth. An adopted male child would, of course, be circumcised—at the earliest possible time if he is over the age of eight days. If he has been circumcised already as a sanitary measure in a hospital's standard procedure, he should be blessed in the synagog and a name given to him, but the Orthodox practice of shedding a single drop of blood is dispensed with. A female adopted child would be named in the temple as the daughter of her parents.

Mixed Marriage

A child of an intermarriage, where the father is an unconverted Gentile, is blessed in the synagog just as would any other Jewish baby.

This is true for a child born out of wedlock, whether the father is Jewish or non-Jewish. If the mother of a child is a non-converted Gentile and her husband is a Jew and they wish the child raised a Jew, the baby would be blessed as usual, but the rabbi would confer with the mother before the ceremony. He would impress her with her obligation to rear the child as a Jew. Although the child will be recognized as a Jew by Liberal Jews and Liberal synagogs and for purposes of *aliyah,* immigration, by the State of Israel, it must clearly be recognized that our Orthodox brethren do not agree. To them the child, no matter how raised, no matter how loyal to Judaism, must be converted before being counted as a Jew. The conversion period will be made much briefer, the ceremony facilitated, but until such a formal ceremony takes place they will not be satisfied.

Teach them diligently to your children

Children

Even the younger children would not be left behind when the family went to the synagog, but they went along as well, in order that they might become accustomed to the mitzvot.

Sɪғʀᴇ ᴛᴏ Dᴇᴜᴛᴇʀᴏɴᴏᴍʏ 31:12;
quoted in L. I. Newman, *Talmudic Anthology,* p. 70

Every people has its lullabies; the Jewish cradle songs were unique in their emphasis on piety and the love of wisdom. *Die beste schora ist das Torah.* "The best merchandise is the Torah," sang the mother to her baby. So from his earliest days was the Jewish child bent to know our path of life.

A lovely old custom was to weigh a child on each birthday and donate a sum proportionate to his gain in weight to charity, especially a fund for scholars.

As the child grew he was immersed in a Jewish atmosphere that was more real in determining the direction of his life than even his rigorous schooling. He savored the flavor of Judaism, the peace of Sabbath serenity, the festive spirit of the holidays. Enraptured, he listened to *Kiddush* and *Havdalah,* and early learned to respond with hearty amen—and received his own tiny sip of wine. He looked with glistening eyes at the Chanukah candles, fondled his store of nuts, twirled his dreidel, and was happy for eight consecutive nights. Passover with its *sedarim* was exciting even though he fell asleep over his thimble of wine long before the *Haggadah* was finished.

25

The proper training of children has always been a foremost concern of Judaism. The first free education for all children of the community seems to have been a Jewish innovation two thousand years ago. Raising a child without training him for a vocation is tantamount to teaching him to be a thief, said the rabbis (*Tosefta* to *Kiddushin* 1, quoted in *Rabbinic Anthology,* p. 444).

An aura of Jewishness is as important today as it ever was for our forebears. The Reform Jewish home should provide the early start that makes our children conscious of the beauties of their religion even before they are ready for school. Not only should they enjoy the holidays at home, they should attend the synagog with their parents. Most temples have family or children's services, and the young worshiper can find delight in the familiar beauties and experiences of his own temple.

The Sabbath and the holidays provide the obvious time to practice Judaism's customs and ceremonies with our children. Judaism's ethic and spirit are of course the motivations of our entire lives. But Reform Jews have long understood that emotion and ceremony cannot be divorced from religion. It is many years since early Reformers attempted to excise all ritual. The trend to foster intellect at the expense of sentiment proved a blind alley. Both we know are needed for a rounded Jewish life.

Yet every Liberal rabbi hears protests from some congregant at his suggestion to reintroduce some lovely rite into the home. There are people who are reluctant to allow a home ceremony, though their objections usually will not stand the test of unemotional thinking.

A frequent source of protest is that ceremony is akin to truckling to Orthodoxy, if not an actual return. People have protested the idea of Bat Mitzvah, calling it a reversion to Orthodoxy, without realizing that no female is ever called to

Our children will be our sureties

the Torah in the traditional synagog—of such irrationalism are these fears compounded.

Part of the protest at the reintroduction of home ritual is that some parents feel uncomfortable as a performer of a religious act. This need present no difficulty. A youngster enjoys being the parent's surrogate and pronouncing a grace or benediction, lighting candles or chanting the *Kiddush*. Thereby parents of an enthusiastic child have their own religious horizons broadened and their Jewish bonds affirmed. The pride and approval of his parents are the reward and continuing motivation for the child.

Books, Books, Books

Every Jewish home should have as its cornerstone an excellent library. A Jewish Publication Society Bible, with its translation done by Jews for Jews, is only the beginning. The Union Prayer Books, the Union Book of Prayers for Home, history books, books on Jewish ethics and Jewish life, on modern Israel, story and picture books, all should be as readily available in the home as their American counterparts. A simple but good Jewish encyclopedia, a commentary on the Bible, Jewish magazines for adult and for child, these should be natural to the Jewish home and the Jewish child.

Prayers in Childhood

Train a child in the way he should go, and when he is old he will not depart from it.

PROVERBS 22:6

Our Orthodox brethren say: "I have set the Lord before me at all times" (Psalms 16:8) and try to live by these words. The round of *mitzvot* (originally "commandments," but now incorporating the idea of good deeds as well) kept the traditional Jew constantly aware of the way to walk with God. These were time-tested instruments of piety which encased the Jew in a framework of sanctity. All the routines of life, from putting on one's shoes to *kashering* a chicken, to the way one stood during certain prayers, had their rules and their role in the pilgrimage to holiness.

We who are Reform Jews find such religious minutiae do not add to our sense of holiness nor make us better persons or Jews. Yet perhaps some of us have cut ourselves off too much from rites and customs that add meaning and color to our lives and those of our children.

So a simple morning prayer to help start our youngsters off is in order. A night prayer will help compose them for sleep and express their thanks for the day. The prayer habit is one of custom and imitation. The blessing over the bread, the *Motzi,* spoken before each meal, helps consecrate the table and its food. The Reform short version of *benschen,* grace after meals, should be used at least after the evening family meal. Started early, our children can continue to dedicate meaningful moments of devotion throughout their lives.

The Name of God

Traditional Jews are wary about writing the name of God, whether in Hebrew or in the vernacular. The name of God is holy in any form, and paper upon which it appears partakes of this holiness and may not be thrown away. Therefore they will not write His name fully but rather write G-d, L-rd, etc. Liberal Jews while respecting the name of God do not feel that a piece of paper becomes holy nor that disposing of it, even though God's name is written upon it, is sacrilege.

Our rabbis used to say

The Religious School

Synagogs and schools are Israel's fortresses.
Shimon ben Lakish, BABA BATRA 8a

The Hebrew word for education is *chinuch,* which is the root word of *chanukah,* dedication. Jewish education should be the dedication of the child to the highest ideals of life. Through the centuries the Jewish school was the prime and usually the only school for the child.

Our children attend secular schools. Even the private schools are for the most part secular in orientation. This is right, for the teaching of religion to children of many religions is difficult if not hazardous—and the separation of church and state is an important principle.

We must supplement our children's secular schooling with religious training to prepare them for living as mature, responsible Jews. Most congregations consider the training of the child as a principal object. In recent years our religious schools have increased the length of the school day and term, and markedly increased standards. The age of Confirmation has been raised and some congregations have equated Confirmation with high school graduation. Many have developed a high school following Confirmation that trains young men and women at a most educable age. From their ranks come the congregational leaders, the rabbis and teachers of tomorrow.

31

The time to begin religious school comes when the child is ready to absorb some of the training, kindergarten. In the days of the *shtetl* the age to begin school was four or five, and a most important time it was. In his newest suit and with the exclamations of joy of his parents and grandparents, the child was conducted to the *cheder,* the one-room school. There, the teacher offered his congratulations on this happy event. The boy was invited to lick off the honey from the page of a Hebrew primer which had been smeared with the sweet stuff. As he did so, his father dropped a few pennies in front of the astonished pupil. "Learning is sweet, and the angels reward the good scholar," was the explanation.

Consecration

There is a Reform ceremony which is a lineal descendant of the pennies of the *shtetl.* Most congregations find joy in the Consecration of new religious school pupils, usually at Simchat Torah. Some congregations also have a kind of Consecration at the close of a pupil's formal religious school education.

The Consecration of the beginning students finds its actual roots in the old tradition of calling children of pre-Bar Mitzvah age to the reading of the Torah at Simchat Torah. In the Orthodox synagog the boys all ascend the *bimah* in a horde, and as some elders hold a *talit* high over all their heads, the benedictions are recited, the Torah portion read, and they are blessed. Then they are rewarded with candy and a flag with an apple mounted on its rod, and sometimes a candle mounted on the apple.

Reform's custom includes the girls as well as the boys, of course, and each youngster ascends the *bimah* for Consecration at the beginning of the first year of attendance. The rabbi charges the group and, resting his hand on each bowed head, he invokes God's blessing. It is a moving moment in their lives and the lives of their parents. It is a reminder to them that their studies at religious school are different in kind from those of their weekday classes.

Curriculum

When the student in the *cheder* had mastered the letters of the alphabet, he was introduced to the study of the Pentateuch. But he did not begin with the sublime dignity of the opening pages of Genesis, or the warm human stories of Abraham or Joseph. He began with Leviticus, the study of ritual, of sacrifices, of purity and impurity. "Let the pure child come to the study of the pure," was the dictum. Soon he was seated in the circle of his fellows, chanting the words of Scripture, translating them into sing-song Yiddish, until the words and the melodies were engraved on his mind.

In this country the reading of the Hebrew of the prayer book displaced the Torah as the prime study in most traditional schools. As the time allotted for Jewish education was reduced, for the major portion of the day was spent at the secular school, the emphasis was laid on the skills that would allow the pupil to participate in the traditional prayer service. Not often was much energy spent in learning to understand the meaning of the prayers. This emphasis on the mechanical aspects of the study of Hebrew and participation in worship resulted in the so-called "lost generation," those who never learned more than how to *daven,* to pray rapidly and, alas, without comprehension.

The modern Liberal Jewish school emphasizes other aspects of Judaism, its history, philosophy, ethical teachings, the word and spirit of the Scriptures and post-biblical literature, our customs and ceremonies, to help form a rounded Jewish education. As the time for all these subjects is necessarily limited, some area must be skimped. Often this is the study of Hebrew, for the study of any language demands more hours a week than many students have for additional study. The ceremony of Bar Mitzvah, which once was frowned on by Reform purists, is now favored by a considerable majority of Reform Jews and congregations. Obviously the preparation of candidates for this ancient rite must include a worthwhile amount of Hebrew study.

Bar Mitzvah

Bar Mitzvah is an old ceremony, just how old no one knows. There are no talmudic references to it. Probably a boy was summoned to the reading of the Torah whenever he was deemed capable. Almost every boy participated as almost all could read, a proud boast. By the time the ceremony became a recorded historical fact, in the Middle Ages, there were mild festivities that followed, featuring a *derashah,* a discourse on the Talmud or Scriptures. Yet Bar Mitzvah was so unimportant in Ashkenazic communities that a boy did not begin to put on a *talit,* a prayer shawl, until he was married. The Sephardim allowed the Bar Mitzvah to don his *talit.*

The words Bar Mitzvah mean Son of the Commandment. They refer to the fact that the boy who is called for the first time to the reading of the Torah was considered old enough to understand the commandments, the *mitzvot,* and be responsible for their fulfillment. He was considered a member of the congregation and began to wear *tefilin,* phylacteries, and be counted in the *minyan,* the quorum necessary for extended divine services.

There is an amusing custom in Morocco where the Bar Mitzvah takes place on a Thursday. After the ceremony the boy recites a *derashah,* an address, showing his Hebraic and talmudic knowledge. He then parades with his open *tefilin* bag among the guests who reward him with gifts of money. He then hands the sum with his thanks to his teacher!

In the traditional synagog, Bar Mitzvah takes places on a Monday or Thursday morning or at the Sabbath morning service. It may also take place on festival mornings or the day of *Rosh Chodesh,* the New Moon, as these are days when the Torah is read. In Liberal congregations a Bar Mitzvah on any morning but the Sabbath would be rare. Some congregations, especially those which have a Torah reading as part of their Friday evening services, allow the ceremony then. Any other time would be inappropriate.

The Bar Mitzvah Service

The Bar Mitzvah ceremony itself has a time-patina'd beauty and can awaken strong emotions in people unrelated to the boy. The youngster's share in the reading of the service varies so much from temple to temple that it is impossible to state what amount of participation is considered standard. It may vary from the recital of the blessings before and after the Torah reading to the complete reading of the Torah, *Haftarah* (prophetic portion) and the entire service as well. Many congregations delight in having the boy serve as precentor for much of the service. Others, especially the larger temples, where there are two and even three boys becoming Bar Mitzvah almost every Sabbath, are satisfied to have a rabbi and cantor present the service as usual, and the Bar Mitzvah boy or boys take part only in the Torah and *Haftarah* reading.

For millennia Jewish boys learned the Torah according to age-old tunes, a method of study based on the knowledge that it is easier for most people to remember a text when set to a chant. It became the practice to teach the Bible according to definite patterns of melody, known as the *trop*. There are two general patterns, one for the Torah, the other for the Prophets, with special *trops* for some books, such as Lamentations and Song of Songs. Printed Hebrew Bibles still include these musical symbols, with the diacritical marks inserted above or below the letters of the text. In many Reform temples the biblical portion is read, not chanted. Under the influence of the He-

From Zion shall go forth the Torah

brew Union College School of Sacred Music, there are now congregations which permit and even encourage the chanting according to the *trop*.

The Age of the Bar Mitzvah

The usual age of Bar Mitzvah is thirteen, although in Reform congregations the date may be postponed. So a boy whose birth date falls in the summer may have his Bar Mitzvah in the fall, or a winter date may be put off till the spring. The Orthodox do not delay a Bar Mitzvah except for serious illness. Their reasons for not delaying are two. First, until a boy is Bar Mitzvah he is not counted in the *minyan,* the quorum needed for extended religious services. The other is that according to religious law the father is responsible for the boy's sins until his Bar Mitzvah. At an Orthodox Bar Mitzvah the father recites a blessing which thanks God for his relinquishment of this responsibility and being freed from any punishment for his son's sinning. As Liberal Judaism does not believe that the Bar Mitzvah ceremony frees the parents of any responsibilities for their son, there is no reason for refusing to postpone briefly a Bar Mitzvah when circumstances so dictate.

Orthodox synagogs will allow a boy to become Bar Mitzvah at the age of twelve if his father is dead, so that he can begin to recite the *Kaddish* prayer that much sooner. As Reform Judaism does not look at the *Kaddish* prayer with the same eyes as does Orthodoxy, this advancing the age for Bar Mitzvah is not usual in Reform. Reform Judaism agrees with *Pirke Avot,* that thirteen is the age "for the commandments" (5:24).

The Derashah

The American variant of the European *derashah* or speech is happily passing. No longer does a youngster arise to state that he is now a man. The *derashah* as originally conceived was the most important part of the ceremony, for it afforded the boy the opportunity to prove his talmudic learning before the congregation. This he would demonstrate by explaining a difficult passage, and if he was sharp enough, offer his own new interpretation, a *chiddush*.

Relatively few boys in this country have studied enough Talmud by the age of thirteen to demonstrate their proficiency in public, so the mere peroration of the old Bar Mitzvah exordium, the thanking of the parents and teachers, became the entire speech. Liberal congregations hear the boy recite a prayer of gratitude and aspiration or an essay on a Jewish theme, as original as the mental efforts of the boy will permit.

In some congregations the father or the boy recites the *Shehecheyanu* blessing, thanking God for sustaining him to this memorable day. In some, the father will rest his hand on his son's head or shoulder and bless him before the ark.

Bat Mitzvah

Although there is supposedly no double standard in Liberal Judaism, with reports of women congregational presidents and officers, their presence in a *minyan,* there is still a long way to go before all remnants of women's ancient disabilities are forgotten. So not all congregations permit Bat Mitzvah, Daughter of the Commandment, ceremony. There is no pertinent reason why a girl should not be accorded every privilege the temple accords to our sons. So any girl of thirteen whose training is sufficient should be allowed to take part in the Torah and worship service—and that is exactly what Bar or Bat Mitzvah consists of.

Whether Bar or Bat Mitzvah, it is an individual achievement which when properly approached and prepared for can be a thrilling experience for the boy or girl and for his or her family. The boy or girl stands alone before the ark, nay, even before God, and leads the congregation in prayer. It may be the only time they do so in life, or it may be the first of many times. A Jewish boy or girl has demonstrated his or her worth and dedication.

The Festivities

One aspect of the traditional Bar Mitzvah we might all emulate was the mildness of the festivities. No elaborate functions, but rather a bit of *branfen,* brandy, and cake and wine would be provided for the worshipers. Dinner for the visiting family members would follow. The accent was distinctly on the religious and educational aspects of the occasion. Presents were few besides the *tefilin, siddur* and embroidered bag to contain them. The boy would offer his *derashah* after the meal and receive the *derashah geschenk,* the sermon gifts. These were usually small sums of money.

The sumptuary laws advocated by a number of temples, restricting the magnitude of the banquets, are completely in the spirit of the religious ceremony. A Bar Mitzvah is not the time to repay social debts or to invite the business world. It is an honored achievement on the part of the boy and a family celebration. Undue ostentation is alien to its spirit.

Bar Mitzvah and Confirmation

A frequent question concerns the difference between Bar Mitzvah and Confirmation, especially since many simple books on Judaism equate the two, as though one were the translation of the other. They are two similar but separate ceremonies, which exist side by side. Confirmation was originally designed to supplant the older custom. In Reform, Bar Mitzvah has had a new lease on life, for the two ceremonies answer different emotional and religious calls.

Bar Mitzvah is an individual or family affair, whereas Confirmation is a group affair, one for the whole congregation. Bar

Mitzvah is the demonstration by the aspirant that he has reached a chronological and educational level where he is able to lead the service as well as participate as a member of the congregation. His performance is an individual one, standing before the congregation.

Confirmation is a group ceremony, though each confirmand feels an individual challenge. Its basic nature is intellectual and spiritual, affirming individual commitment to Judaism. Confirmation requires dedication and study on a high level, and as such is the preferable if there is to be only the one ceremony. But this is not to deny the validity and value and impact of Bar Mitzvah.

Confirmation

Confirmation comes later than Bar Mitzvah and this alone is evidence of its value, for additional time to study with increased maturity is of priceless worth in the education of our young people. The study of Judaism is too important, too profound to be terminated at Bar Mitzvah age. If one rejoins that even sixteen is insufficient, the answer is that only lifelong study will really suffice.

Confirmation as introduced by the early German Reform Jew Israel Jacobson, in Seesen in 1810, was based on the somewhat similar ceremony of the Protestant church. He sought to supplant Bar Mitzvah with this new rite as an affirmation of the truth of the faith of Israel. He felt that Bar Mitzvah, with its accent on the reading of the blessings, the Torah and *Haftarah,* did not provide the child the necessary opportunity to voice his own understanding of Judaism and to express his loyalty to its teachings.

In 1817 in Berlin, girls as well as boys appeared before the congregation to mark a religious affirmation of Judaism. Slowly the new custom evolved until it is now almost as common in Conservative congregations as it is in Reform, and is important for girls in many Orthodox congregations. It has become firmly related to the Festival of Shavuot with its dual celebration of First Fruits and the Giving of the Torah on Sinai. So our young people, these first and best of our fruits, accept their responsibility in Judaism on the same day that Israel accepted God's Torah in mutual covenant.

By unanimous resolution the Central Conference of American Rabbis has affirmed that Confirmation takes place on the eve or the day of Shavuot. Some small congregations move the date to the nearest Sabbath or even to Sunday. Of course this deprives the occasion of its full meaning.

Its Meaning

Confirmation means that the aspirants affirm their faith in the religion of Israel and in God. This requires them to have come to some measure of understanding of Judaism. The rabbi or confirmation teachers deliberately promote a seeking, searching spirit in the confirmands. No longer are they to be content to be Jews because of birth; they must learn deeper reasons that will equip them to form a mature understanding. They must study the bases of Judaism, the meaning of the Jewish idea of God, of prayer, of ethics. Then they must study the religions of their neighbors and how they relate to Judaism. They must be familiar with our prayer service, its history and its meaning. They must have learned the history of their people and the development of modern Judaism and Reform Judaism in particular. Then and only then are they ready to stand before the congregation and vow that they are truly Jews, based on their study and their understanding and their own personal loyalty to Judaism. Thus Confirmation should be the culmination of a student's years of attendance at religious school, a spiritual quest finding direction and guidance if not always precise answers.

Engagement and Marriage

Happy is the man who has a good wife!
The number of his days is doubled.
A worthy wife gladdens her husband,
And he lives out his years in peace.
BEN SIRA 26:1,2

Marriage is the natural state of man, according to Jewish teaching. "It is not good for a man to be alone," said the Lord God, "I will make a fitting helper for him" (Genesis 2:18). At no time in Jewish life has it been considered a virtue to remain unmarried. Chastity, yes; celibacy, no! Even the cynical Koheleth said, "Enjoy life with the wife whom you love all the days of the life of your vanity, which He has given you under the sun" (Ecclesiastes 9:9).

Arranged Marriages

Until recently most Jewish marriages were arranged. The role of *shadchan*, matchmaker, is an old if not always honored profession. Yet we have knowledge of eminent rabbis and community leaders who considered it fitting to earn a living by arranging suitable marriages for a fee. The criteria for a proper match had little to do with wealth. Most estimable of all was *yichus*, pedigree, and this referred to a background of rabbis and scholars. The daughter of a talmudic sage was considered a far better catch than that of the wealthiest man. And a young man of learning was sought after by the agents

43

of the richest merchants, who vied with each other to promise him a life with endless opportunity to study.

According to tradition, the girl had the right to refuse the groom, based on the biblical tale of Rebecca and Laban and the servant of Abraham: "Let us call the girl and ask for her reply" (Genesis 24:57). So too the Talmud states, "A man is forbidden to betroth his daughter while she is a minor. She must wait until she is of age and will say, 'This is the man of my choice'" (*Kiddushin* 42a).

And we find the converse, "A man is forbidden to betroth a woman until he sees her, lest he later find in her a blemish and then she repel him" (*ibid.*).

In older times, and among Oriental Jews even now, there was a *mohar* or bridal price. This was the gift of the groom's family and an obvious replacement of the ancient bridal purchase. There was also the *natan,* a gift to the bride of jewelry or raiment, from the groom and his family. Although the *mohar* technically belonged to the bride's father, he more often turned most or all of it over to his daughter. Gradually the *mohar* was transformed from a purchase price to a bridal gift. Even more important, the bride gained rights to personal property.

The Dowry

The custom of a bridal gift or dowry is very ancient. Until very recently the *nadan* or *nedunya,* the dowry, was a major factor in the planning of a wedding. Even a girl possessing *yichus,* pedigree, and beauty who lacked a fair sum to enable her and a mate to get started in life might have great difficulty in finding a match. An average girl might even have to give up hope. So fundamental was the need for *nadan* that societies called *hachnasat kallah* were set up whose sole purpose was to raise funds to supply poor girls with the few hundred rubles or thalers or scudi they needed to marry. Israel's Nobel prize winning author, S. J. Agnon, in his *Marriage Canopy*, tells the tale of a man who wanders the Jewish world seeking contributions to supply his daughters with a *nadan*.

If the father had some money of his own and wished a scholar as a son-in-law, he might offer *kest* as part of the *nadan*. This was the promise to support the *yeshivah bachur* as a student for a period of years. The young man could thus continue his studies without worry. This is still true of chasidic Jews today.

Modern variants of the *nadan* and *kest* have evolved to fit individual needs, though without the formal recognition the older customs possessed.

Ketubah

In the period of the Second Commonwealth, the *ketubah*, the marriage contract, came into existence. This document was the bride's protection. It changed the *mohar* or purchase price into a lien, to be paid by the husband in case of divorce, or by his heirs in case of his death. Rabbi Shimon ben Shatach declared that the *mohar*, which was ordinarily 200 silver dinars for a virgin and 100 for a widow, should not actually be paid—but written in the *ketubah*. The wife would receive the specified sum if she was divorced or on her husband's death.

Rabbi Shimon's significant reform made marriage easier, as the groom did not need 200 or even 100 dinars in cash to purchase a bride. But he did need this sum to divorce. So the *ketubah* helped protect women from impulsive divorces.

In itself, *ketubah* is a legal document written in Aramaic, the language of the common people of 2000 years ago. Hebrew had already become the tongue of study and prayer alone. And the rabbis wished to be sure that the common man understood the terms of this important undertaking. The protecting *ketubah* was subject to only one change. The specified sums were to be increased when the bride came from a priestly or rabbinic or aristocratic family. This made divorce even more difficult. A woman could not even live with her husband without her *ketubah*. It was her protection. If lost or burned, he had to leave home until a new *ketubah* could be written and signed.

Incidentally, Sephardic *ketubot* contain a clause that the husband may not take a second wife without the permission of his first. In the eleventh century the edict of Rabbenu Gershom, the Light of the Exile, forbade Ashkenazic Jews a second wife, even with the permission of the first. The Sephardim do not recognize the validity of Gershom's *takanah,* and so are legally entitled to plural marriages. When Oriental Jews from Arab lands come to the new state of Israel, they sometimes bring with them two or more wives. Israeli law states: If a man has two wives wedded to him in a land where such marriages are legal according to both the law of the land and Jewish law, he may retain both. If he is one of the very few who has married a third as well, he has to choose amongst them as only two are considered legal in Israel. But once settled in Israel, no one, not even a Sephardic Jew, may take two wives without incurring the penalty of bigamy.

Scripture lists various relatives whom it is prohibited to espouse. The Talmud added to the list. Liberal Judaism respects this listing and abides by it, and Reform rabbis do not take part in such marriages.

Conversely, even if Jewish law does permit a certain type of marriage which state law prohibits—i.e., an uncle to his niece—no rabbi may perform such a ceremony, as "the law of the land is the law" (*Baba Kamma* 113a).

(See Appendix for list of prohibited marriages.)

Levirate Marriage

Levirate marriage is based on an old custom, still respected by the Orthodox. A man who died without progeny had no one

May the Holy One bless our bridegroom and his bride

to say *Kaddish* for him, no one to carry on his name. So it was determined that his brother should marry the bereft wife, and the first born would be considered the son of the dead brother. The brother could refuse to marry his sister-in-law, but he had to go through a humiliating ceremony, for it was felt that he had let down his dead brother.

Until the brother either married the widow or went through with the ceremony that relieved him of this duty, *chalitzah,* the widow was prohibited from marrying at all. If the brother was too young either to marry or to go through the rite of *chalitzah,* she had to wait until he reached the age of puberty, in early days—or his Bar Mitzvah, today. If there was no brother, the nearest male relative had to assume the obligation. Since a formal decision by American Reform rabbis in 1868 in Philadelphia, neither levirate marriage nor *chalitzah* has any currency for Liberal Jews.

Betrothal

The betrothal was termed *erusin,* a joining. It was a binding contract that only a formal divorce could dissolve. Later this strictness disappeared so that a divorce was not involved. Yet the Gaon of Vilna declared that if a couple broke their engagement, they could never marry—which was even more stringent than if they had been married and divorced, for then they could remarry. His purpose was to do away with the casual breaking of engagements.

In Orthodox circles the *tenaim,* the agreement to and the signing of the engagement contract, still constitute a formal and important step. But the actual *erusin,* ritual of engagement, has been joined to the ritual of marriage, so that both take place at the marriage ceremony—which is the reason why there are two separate cups of wine and two blessings over the wine at a traditional wedding.

There is no formal religious ceremony among **Reform Jews** at the time of engagement, nor is there any if an engagement is broken.

The Date

Among all Jews, weddings do not take place on the festivals (Purim and Chanukah do not count as festivals), or on the Sabbath. There are two reasons: The first is that a wedding is a binding of a contract, and no business is done on the Sabbath or festivals. The other reason is that we are not supposed to mix two *simchot,* two joyous occasions. Each demands its own fulfillment. So traditional Jews will not marry off two children of the same family on one day. Each deserves the right to be the center of the day's joy.

Orthodox Jews add to the list of restricted days all fast days of the Jewish calendar, plus the period between Pesach and Shavuot (except for Lag Ba-Omer and the New Moon, which are permissible days), and from the seventeenth of Tamuz through the first nine days of the month of Av. As the explanations relating to these two periods seem compounded mainly of superstition, Liberal Jews consider themselves free to marry during these periods. But they do not marry on the ninth of Av, as it is the day of mourning for the destruction of the Temples.

It was not customary to marry on the *chol ha-moed,* the intermediary days of a festival, nor on the eve of a festival, but Orthodox law does allow a man to remarry his divorced wife then. Liberal Jews may marry on the *chol ha-moed* or the eve of a festival, as the restrictions have only to do with the preparation for the festivities.

There are some authorities who do not allow marriages during the Ten Days of Repentance, the first ten days of the month of Tishri. But even Orthodox custom is not consistent here. So Liberal Jews may marry then, though of course not on Rosh Hashanah or Yom Kippur.

The *Aufruf* is the call to the bridegroom for an *aliyah*, . . . the recitation of the blessings over the Torah, on the Sabbath before the marriage. This custom has been continued in many Liberal congregations. In others, the bride and groom may participate in the *kiddush* and candle blessing. There may also be a prayer of blessing from the pulpit by the rabbi.

The Chupah

All traditional Jews use a *chupah*, either an elaborate canopy suspended on four poles, held above the heads of the bridal pair, or just a *talit* held at each corner by the four tallest men present. Many a soldier-groom remembers his wedding as a battle to see as a buddy's arm weakened and the *talit* fell across his eyes.

Originally, the *chupah* was a pavilion hung with precious tapestries, in the house of the father of the groom. The wood came from trees planted at the birth of the bride and groom. This was the marriage chamber, even in biblical days a remnant of the pastoral era.

By the Middle Ages the custom of leading the bride publicly to the marriage chamber semed obvious. Besides, it was now the groom who went to the house of the bride's father.

In Poland arose the custom of a portable canopy, symbolizing the ancient private chamber. The majority of weddings were held in the *shulehof*, the synagog courtyard. A ceremony held under the shining stars was an omen that the offspring would be as numerous as the stars.

In Reform Judaism the *chupah* is not a necessary adjunct to a marriage, though it is frequently used. It has its decorative as well as its associative aspects. It may be a composition of flowers or an embroidered cloth.

The Banquet for the Poor

A day or two before the wedding a special meal was provided for the poor of the community. The bride and groom were seated at the head-table. The paupers were waited on by the parents and relatives, not by servants. After the meal the couple danced with the poor and coins were distributed. Sh. An-ski's *The Dybbuk* makes much of this reminder to the happy of their duties to their less fortunate relations. In Liberal Judaism the custom is to contribute a generous sum to charity.

The Mikveh

The day before the wedding the bride was accompanied to the *mikveh*, the ritual bath, by her friends. In olden days she was preceded by the *klezmorim*, the musicians. The use of the ritual bath has been dropped completely by Liberal Jews. Yet even today, despite the ease of modern cleanliness at home, Orthodox women use the *mikveh* regularly.

Badekens

A ritual still performed by traditional Jews is the *badekens*, covering the bride's face just before the ceremony. The veil is placed on her head as she is blessed by the rabbi. In some localities the groom participated in this veiling. It is said that he participated to be sure that it was his Rachel and not a substituted Leah who would greet him after the veil was removed. As modern veils are not opaque, Liberal Jews do not hold the *badekens*.

There is a belief among some Jews that the groom and bride should not see each other the day of the wedding until they meet under the *chupah*. There is some slight basis for this belief in the old Orthodox custom of keeping couples apart during their engagement. But as the *badekens* ceremony clearly shows, they would meet before the ceremony. This belief, therefore, must derive from some superstition and has no validity.

Among the Orthodox the bride and groom fast on their wedding day and repent of their sins. This is not a usual custom among Reform Jews.

The Wedding

The bridegroom wears a *talit* at a traditional wedding. The ultra-Orthodox groom also wears a *kittel,* a white robe, which he will wear henceforth on Yom Kippur and at the Pesach *seder,* and in which he will be buried. In Europe, the *talit* would be a bridal gift and the first he owned. Bar Mitzvah came and went and the boy did not look forward to his first *talit* until his wedding approached.

In traditional circles, other participants in the wedding ceremony are the *unterfirers,* married couples who have never been divorced, and who are close friends of the family. They stand somewhat as godparents, and they help the parents accompany the bride and groom to the *chupah.*

In Liberal Judaism the procession no longer contains the *unterfirers* and need not include both parents of the bride and groom as well. Some Liberal Jews still like to have the couple accompanied by their parents, but many prefer both the mothers and the groom's father to be seated before the ceremony begins. The bride comes down the aisle on her father's arm, to be surrendered to her groom, and then the father takes a seat next to his wife in the first row.

Also in limbo is the ancient march of the bride around the groom, seven times, or in some places, only three times. No satisfactory reason has ever been offered for this bit of perambulation. Some say that the custom arose so that the groom may be sure that it is his intended under the veil and not another. Others say that it is so that the bride can view her spouse-to-be closely and decide finally whether to say yes or no. But as the bride will have to lift her veil before the first cup of wine at an Orthodox ceremony, these reasons are hardly satisfying.

The groom always takes his place first, as it would be discourteous to make the bride wait for him. The bride stands at her groom's right: "At your right stands the queen" (Psalms 45:10).

The ceremony may be conducted by any informed male, yet it was almost always performed by the rabbi of the community, who might be assisted by the *chazan,* the cantor, or *shamash,* the sexton. The cantor almost never performed a wedding himself, as its major content is not the chanting of the benedictions, but the wedding's legal character and the moral discourse with which the rabbi charges the bride and groom.

As the reasons for the two glasses of wine used by traditional Jews are connected with outmoded legalisms, Reform Jews use only one. At traditional weddings the groom drinks first and then offers the cup to his bride. In Reform, the groom offers the cup to his bride first.

The Ring

In traditional ceremonies only the groom gives a ring. This is because the marriage was considered a legal contract, and the giving of the ring is a symbol of the *kinyan,* the purchase. If the bride gave her groom a ring in return, there would be no legal purchase.

So, too, the ring used in traditional weddings is always a simple gold hoop. This is often explained as an expression of the wish that the life together of the spouses may be as precious and unimpeded as the ring. Most scholars believe that the insistence on a simple gold ring is related to the idea of *kinyan,* purchase. If there is to be a purchase the ring must have real value, equal to at least five silver pieces. As a rabbi is usually not a jeweler, he can't be expected to know if a ring with stones is valuable or not. But he can heft a ring of gold and recognize by its weight that it is not of brass.

As a marriage is not considered a purchase by Liberal Jews, any ring may be used, preferably the one the bride will wear. So, too, Liberal Jews may have a double ring ceremony.

Also, traditional Jews require that the groom place the ring on the index finger of the right hand of his bride. According to ancient understanding of physiology there was a vein running from this finger right to the heart. Liberal Jews place the ring on the usual finger of the left hand, where it will be worn.

Anyone who has visited a Jewish museum may have a question here. A particularly interesting display in any Jewish museum is the collection of medieval marriage rings from central Europe. These are large silver rings bearing as adornment a small intricately worked house. Each was the property of a local Jewish community and it was used at every wedding. How, then, did the *kinyan* or purchase take place if the ring belonged to the community? The ring was used as a tax device. Each groom had to buy the ring from the community for five silver coins. He then gave it to his bride at the wedding. She would wear it just one day, and then return it as a gift to the community. This charming custom fell into abeyance because of persecution, and the rings that have survived the centuries are now treasured relics of a bygone age.

At a traditional wedding the *ketubah* is read in the original Aramaic. This is to prove to the assemblage that the bride is protected. At some Orthodox weddings today, the *shamash* reads the *ketubah* while the *chazan* or a soloist sings a modern love song.

Liberal rabbis will fill out either the elaborate traditional *ketubah* or a simpler modern wedding certificate. They may or may not read a portion of either document at the wedding.

To Break or Not to Break!

The traditional wedding ends with the groom smashing a glass with one stroke of his right heel—though there are communities where he dashes the glass to the ground from his right hand, and steps on it only if it fails to shatter. And there are others where a plate is used instead of a glass. The origin of this most ancient custom is lost. You may hear tell that it is a sign of mourning for the Temple. There is a recounting in the Talmud of a rabbi who in the midst of the festivities of his son's wedding, hurled a costly glass vase to the floor—to remind his guests of their mortality (*Berachot* 30b). No one really knows whether this is the reason, or whether it is only a propitiation of evil spirits, so they may not be jealous of the unmitigated joy. It has been an integral part of the nuptials for at least two thousand years. Liberal Jews may dispense with this act, if they so prefer.

The festivities after the actual wedding ceremony are as traditional as the ritual itself. They have at times become overly lavish, and we read of medieval sumptuary laws to limit such expenditure. We must always remember that the Hebrew word for the marriage ceremony is *kiddushin,* a making holy.

The practice that after the wedding banquet the *Sheva Berachot,* Seven Benedictions, of the ceremony are repeated as part of the *benschen,* the grace after meals, is not usual among Reform Jews. However, the *Motzi,* the blessing before the meal, is obligatory.

Conversion

He who brings a man under the wings of the Shechinah *is regarded as if he had created him.*

GENESIS RABAH 39:14

Judaism has not been a conversionist religion since the Emperor Constantine, in 315 C.E., decreed the death penalty for anyone who converted to Judaism—and for the person who accepted him into our faith. This remained in rigorous effect through the eighteenth century. Yet it did not stop individuals from converting to the faith of Israel, sometimes even knowing that they would pay for this temerity with their lives. Through the years individuals have come to Judaism of their own volition and their children were as one with the rest of Israel.

Yet Judaism has remained a non-proselytizing religion. This is not because Jews are particularistic, refusing to share their treasure with anyone. Partly it is due to the church's rigorous opposition and fierce reprisal. Even more important, it is because Judaism does not relegate the non-Jew to hell or even to limbo. God's love is sufficient for everyone, and is not reserved for the house of Jacob. As Rabbi Joshua said, "The righteous of all nations shall have a share in the world to come" (*Tosephta Sanhedrin* 13:2, quoted in *Rabbinic Anthology,* p. 604).

The rabbis made a point of this in discussing the story of

57

the Deluge. Noah "walked with God" (Genesis 6:9), yet as he was pre-Abraham he could not be a Jew. Therefore, they reasoned, a non-Jew could serve God. The rabbis asked how did Noah earn God's love. They answered by saying that Noah and his sons observed seven fundamental ethical rules: injunctions against murder, theft, adultery and incest, worship of idols, blasphemy, gross cruelty to animals; and the need to bring disputes to a court of law rather than settling them by force.

These seven are called the natural law and the rabbis termed them the Noahide laws. As Judaism teaches justification by works and not by belief, any human who obeys these seven rules is worthy of God's approbation.

Therefore, we who are Jews must call this simple way to walk before God to the attention of any would-be converts. We must also tell them that they would be leaving the majority religion for a minority religion, one that has known grave persecution (*Yevamot* 47a,b). Yet as we repel with the left hand, we draw near with the right. As the sages said: "As long as he comes in the name of God, for the sake of heaven, befriend him and do not repel him" (*Mechilta,* Lauterbach edition, II, p. 173).

Orthodox Conversion

The Orthodox position on conversion is not so simple as the rabbinic quotation might indicate. Lest a non-Jew ask to be admitted to Judaism for gain or for marriage, most traditional rabbis will not accept him unless he proves he has no ulterior motive whatsoever. This presents difficulties in some instances where marriage to a Jew is contemplated. Happily, most Orthodox rabbis in America have not been rigorous in their acceptance of proselytes. As Orthodox Judaism is not highly structured, if one Orthodox rabbi refuses a candidate, there are many others who will almost certainly accept him.

This is not true in Great Britain, for instance, or in Israel, where a candidate for conversion must prove that he or she does not have marriage in mind as the reason for seeking conversion.

If a person has been converted to Judaism by a Conservative or Liberal rabbi, the conversion is not considered valid by Orthodoxy. This refusal presents a danger to the future of *K'lal Yisrael,* the unity of the whole house of Israel. Converts may live their whole lives as Jews, as members of a congregation, active and ardent in Jewish causes, only to discover that they or their children are not recognized as Jewish by the Orthodox. If the mother in such a union is the born-Jew, the children are recognized as Jewish by the Orthodox. However, if the mother is the convert, the children are not so recognized, and if they wish to have themselves considered part of Orthodox Jewry they must be converted by an Orthodox rabbi.

This presents little problem in American Jewry except for the few who stem from Reform Jewish families and decide to become part of the Orthodox community. Only when the child of a converted mother wishes to marry an Orthodox Jew or join an Orthodox congregation does this problem manifest itself.

The preparation for conversion varies. Some Orthodox rabbis ask only to be convinced of the applicant's sincerity. Others demand a probationary period of a year or even more. However, the actual ceremony of Orthodox conversion is not lengthy. The candidate is probed as to his sincerity. Sometimes he is examined as to his knowledge of the *mitzvot.* Usually he must promise to observe them all, though there are some "neo-Orthodox" rabbis who are satisfied with the profession of knowledge without demanding a vow they know will not be lived up to.

When the presiding rabbi is satisfied the applicant is circumcised. When the wound is healed he is taken to the *mikveh,* ritual bath. A woman has only to be told of the *mitzvot* and enter the *mikveh* and she is accepted. As the new Jew leaves the *mikveh* water he or she pronounces the traditional blessing on bathing in a *mikveh,* for now it is as a full-fledged Jew that the blessing is spoken.

Liberal Conversion

Liberal Judaism insists on a long period of preparation to be sure that the candidate is truly aware of its ethical, spiritual and ceremonial teachings. This may require a few months or even a year, depending on the background of the applicant and other factors. He is required to attend religious services regularly. In large cities his training will probably be in a regular class for converts. In suburban temples the applicant may be asked to attend the adult education classes.

Whether the training is in class or in private session, the emphasis is the same: to assure understanding and fidelity to the faith of Israel. When the rabbi is satisfied with the convert's progress, he arranges for the ceremony. It is brief and it is private. Two Jewish witnesses must be present. Frequently they are two other rabbis, forming a *bet din,* a formal Jewish court. This is not imperative, and any two Jewish adults, often including the president of the congregation, will be sufficient.

The candidate gives evidence of his knowledge of Judaism through a brief question and answer period. Then the formal ceremony, as printed in the *Rabbi's Manual* or another, as arranged by the officiating rabbi, is performed. This includes the renunciation of the former faith, the pledge of fealty to Judaism, the promise to rear any offspring as Jews, to circumcise any male children, and the adoption of a new, biblical name.

Most Reform rabbis do not insist on the circumcision of a male proselyte, as traditional Jews do. Orthodox Jews go so far as to insist on the shedding of one drop of blood if the convert had been circumcised before his conversion. Some Reform Rabbis insist the convert, male or female, be immersed in the *mikveh,* to duplicate traditional procedure. All Reform rabbis in Israel insist on *milah* and *mikveh.*

Once the ceremony is over the convert is considered a *ben* or *bat Avraham Avinu,* a son or daughter of our Father Abraham. They are considered Jews in every sense of the word, and may be called to the Torah, serve as officers of a congregation, as a rabbi or cantor, etc.

A certificate or formal document is given to the convert and a record of the conversion is kept in the temple files. Most Liberal rabbis ask that the convert join the temple.

Traditional Jews deny a marriage between a *kohen,* a descendant of Aaron, and a convert. As the *kohanim* have no priestly function in Reform Judaism, this ban does not hold for us.

Lest any Jew maintain that converts hold a second-class place in the Jewish community, the rabbis warned that any Jew who insulted a convert because of his non-Jewish origin deserved punishment. They said: "The stranger who yields himself to the divine commands is dearer to God even than Israel at Sinai, for he comes without the constraining terror of thunder and lightning, and voluntarily submits himself to one with the Holy One" (*Tanchuma Lech Lecha* 6, Buber ed., 32).

Conversion and Israel

The Israeli government despite the protests of the Orthodox rabbinate recognize Conservative and Liberal conversions made outside the land. Such converts and their children may take full advantage of the Law of Return and be registered as Jews. However, the Orthodox rabbinate refuses to recognize such conversions and insists on a traditional conversion before allowing these people to be married according to *halachah.* As they control all Jewish marriage and there is no civil marriage in Israel, they can make it difficult for those who have undergone less than Orthodox conversion. The non-traditional Jewish community of Israel insists on full recognition of its converts, especially since all is done by the rules of *halachah,* but the Orthodox refuse.

Divorce

"When a man puts aside the wife of his youth, even the very altar weeps."

GITTIN 90b

Divorce has always been possible in Judaism. Though looked upon as a sad happening, it was recognized as at times necessary. Even in early days Jewish divorce had a legal character and the Bible speaks of the necessity for a bill of divorcement (Deuteronomy 24:1). So divorce in Judaism was never as simple as the "I divorce you, I divorce you!" of the Arabs.

Judaism recognizes that though a marriage is a *kiddushin,* a sanctification, an unhappy marriage cannot be considered holy. Better to separate and seek happiness with a new mate or even alone. Two thousand years ago there was a controversy between the great masters of the era, Hillel and Shammai. Shammai would allow divorce only for some strong overriding reason, such as adultery. But Hillel maintained that a man need no reason but that his wife had displeased him. And Hillel's decision prevailed. (See *The Jewish Encyclopedia,* IV, p. 625.)

Yet divorce is never treated lightly in Judaism. There is a whole tractate of the Talmud called *Gittin* dealing with divorce. Despite Hillel's view, divorce was never common among Jews and was always greeted with sadness.

The Torah which the Lord set before Israel

And let us not forget the protection the Jewish woman had in the contractual obligation of the *ketubah,* her marriage document. The husband had to pay her a considerable sum to achieve his freedom. This obligation was specifically devised (a) to keep divorce from becoming frequent, (b) to allow the woman to live without being helpless. With the sum she received she could return to her family and be welcomed, or use it as a dowry and thus more readily find a mate, or invest it and provide for herself.

To further prevent easy divorce and to protect the woman and her children, the sages in the era of the Second Temple set up rabbinic courts, hemmed in by exact legal niceties. The divorce document had to be drawn up most precisely. The financial matters had to be settled and fulfilled to the court's satisfaction. An elaborate ritual was evolved. The *get,* bill of divorcement, had to be written in twelve lines, the numerical equivalent of the word *get,* by a regular scribe. There had to be no confusion as to names. When it was handed to the woman it was taken and torn to signify the complete tearing of the marriage bond—and to ensure that the same writ would not be used for another woman with the same name. All this was done to underline the importance of divorce, so that none might go through the whole ceremony without ample time for reconsideration.

But if the husband truly wanted a divorce and was able to satisfy the financial settlement, he could always obtain it. The woman was not in the same position. She was protected from being thrust out penniless and homeless. Yet she could not instigate divorce proceedings. The law said that she could if her husband contracted leprosy or he was flagrantly immoral. But in practice, it was very rare that a woman could obtain a divorce without a husband's cooperation. If he was unfaithful, failed to provide for her, or did not perform his conjugal duty, the rabbinic court would endeavor to force him to divorce her. But if they could not, she was in a difficult situation. She could only try to induce him—or bribe him to divorce her.

This double standard has persisted in traditional Judaism until this day, so that many Orthodox rabbis are troubled. However, the problem is not easily removed as technically a solution can only be reached by formal action of a *Sanhedrin,* the rabbinical legislature of a bygone era. The convocation of a *Sanhedrin* today is prevented because there are serious questions as to the modern ordination of rabbis, that is, whether there is a direct chain linking them to the rabbis of the Second Commonwealth.

The rabbis of Israel have been pressed to convoke a *Sanhedrin,* but they refused. They did deal, though hesitantly, with one of the other most serious difficulties concerning marriage and divorce, the *agunah.*

The Agunah

There is no Enoch Arden law in Jewish tradition. A man who has left home had better arrange to die with two witnesses near, or his widow is in serious and sometimes unsolvable trouble. And the witnesses have to be both male and Jewish. If the husband has been killed before a whole army corps of non-Jews and buried with high military honors—by non-Jews, all of whom are willing to swear to his death, it still would not help his widow. By Jewish law, she is still his wife.

Or if he were drowned before an assemblage of Jewish women and his body did not reappear, the story is the same.

Some Orthodox rabbis softened the need for two male Jewish witnesses: one Jew and a gentile would suffice. But basically there was no change in the law until after the Hitler holocaust when thousands of Jewish women found themselves alive at the end of the war, but husbandless and prohibited from remarriage. After arduous pressure and threats of mass-suicide, the rabbis of Israel finally decided that the genocide of the war was such that it could be equated with the case of a man entering a lion's den and not emerging, or a man cast overboard in the presence of sharks. So any man caught up in the war who did not return to his wife was presumed dead, and his widow was given the right to remarry.

Ordinarily, Orthodox Jews on their going to war or on a long and dangerous journey, give their wives provisional divorces. But World War II caught up millions who did not have the chance to provide such provisional writs.

The problem of the deserted wife, the *agunah,* has not been satisfactorily settled in Israel or anywhere among Orthodox Jews. Conservative Jews enter into the *ketubah,* the marriage contract, the provision that if the husband leaves his wife for a certain number of years and does not return or communicate with her in any way, it is understood that he meant to divorce her.

Similarly, Conservative Jews have tried to legislate counselling where the marriage does not seem to be working, by specifying that the couple must consult with a rabbi before they seek divorce. However, this codicil has no legal value, and if it has been effective it has been because of the spiritual influence of the couple's rabbi. Orthodox rabbis refuse to allow this provision to be added to the *ketubah,* because they will not change the traditional form.

Liberal Jews agree that when the civil courts declare a missing spouse dead, he or she must be considered dead by any reasonable standard. Therefore the survivor is free to marry without any religious declaration or need for attestation.

If the survivor is a male, there can be no real difficulty even with the most Orthodox—for men traditionally were allowed a second wife, and even though there is a venerable *takanah* against plural marriage, the new marriage is at most venial and no guilt rests upon the new wife or the children of the new match. But if the survivor is the wife, the Orthodox aver that the civil court's declaration is not sufficient to free her; a rabbinic court must so pronounce. If witnesses cannot be found to satisfy the rabbinic court, they will refuse to so declare, and thus she will be prohibited from marriage, and if she does wed the progeny are *mamzerim,* bastards, and may not enter the traditional Jewish community.

Happily, this is a rare instance and will affect very few, but it points out Liberal Judaism's acceptance of civil law and Orthodoxy's reluctance, even though the Talmud says the law of the land is the law.

The Law of the Land

Liberal Judaism finds no difficulty with either of these major problems of Orthodoxy, the *agunah* or the problem of wives not being able to institute divorce proceedings. According to the Talmud, *dina demalchuta dina,* the law of the land is the law (*Baba Kamma* 113a). So even the most Orthodox Jews will not seek or grant a divorce until the civil court grants it first. This order of precedence does not arise in modern Israel, for there all matters of marriage and divorce are settled by Jewish law in Jewish rabbinic courts, except in the most unusual circumstances. Muslims and Christians have their own ecclesiastical courts for all such matters. Every person in Israel is considered to be a member of a religious *millet,* or denomination, and his marital life is determined by the internal religious law of his *millet.* Even Liberal Jews are subject to Orthodox rabbinic law in Israel.

Lest this seem singularly unfair, please be reminded that every land has its own law concerning marriage and divorce. And this law holds good for Jews as well as the majority denomination—unlike Israel, where each person is governed by his own denomination and not that of the majority. So Jews who live in Spain or Portugal cannot divorce at all, as these governments, because of church pressure, prohibit divorce for all their subjects, Jews and Protestants as well as Roman Catholics. The couple can go to France and get a divorce, but if either remarries he cannot return to their native land—for there it would be considered bigamy.

But in countries where there is divorce, the law of the land prevails. This means that Jews who observe traditional law yet must observe the marriage and divorce laws of their state. Therefore, before an Orthodox or Conservative Jew can even apply for a religious divorce from a rabbinic court in the United States or in England or France or wherever civil divorce is legal, he must first obtain a civil divorce. Once this divorce is granted, the rabbinic court will almost automatically issue the religious decree upon proper application. The ancient legal forms are followed, but they no longer have any restraining force. Even the provision for moneys to the wife is no longer respected, except in ultra-Orthodox circles, for the sums are meaningless today, and the civil courts take care of alimony or cash settlement, custody of any children, provisions for their upkeep, etc.

This loss of meaning of the terms of the *ketubah* is why most Liberal rabbis not only do not require a Jewish divorce before they will marry a divorced person to a new mate, they may well refuse to issue any sort of divorce paper even when asked for it. Some Liberal rabbis will issue a statement certifying the applicant's legal and religious status concerning divorce and the right to remarry. Those who do so maintain that it is a Reform version of the old writ of divorce, and that it is a real satisfaction to the persons involved. Such a Reform *get* has no value to traditional Jews.

Those rabbis who will not issue such a certificate say that it is not a meaningful substitute for a *get,* and as it has no validity in Jewish law it is only a sop for the nostalgic.

Orthodox Versus Non-Orthodox Divorce

This question of Jewish divorce militates against the future of *K'lal Yisrael,* catholic Israel, the whole house of Jewry as a religion. According to the Orthodox, a woman with only a secular divorce is still married to her first husband. She is considered living in sin with her new paramour, whom she may think is her husband. She may think herself married to this new man, she may even have had a Liberal rabbi perform the ceremony. He may have given her a *ketubah*. But any children she may bear will be illegitimate. These children, the Orthodox aver, though legal according to civil law, are considered bastards. They may not marry another Jew except another bastard, for "a bastard shall not enter into the assembly of the Lord" (Deuteronomy 23:3).

Obviously Reform Jews will not consider such children outside the pale, and will consider them legitimate and completely marriageable. This difficult situation is even more threatening because the Orthodox not only refuse to recognize any Liberal marriages of the divorced to new mates, they also refuse the divorces issued by the Conservative *bet din,* court of rabbinic law. Though the Conservative movement has been careful that their rabbis who serve as *dayanim,* judges, in such divorce courts are most knowledgeable, that the forms are fulfilled precisely as minutely described in the Talmud and by later rabbis, yet the Orthodox declare their decisions invalid. And any children born to a woman so divorced, though with all the niceties of Jewish law, and though remarried with *chupah* and *ketubah,* are considered absolutely and irrevocably illegitimate.

The reason that only the woman's children are so branded is that according to ancient Jewish law a man may have plural wives. It is true that Rabbenu Gershom a thousand years ago proscribed polygamy and that his decision holds for all Western Jews. But his edict does not brand the children of a second marriage of a male without divorce. The father is told not to remarry without a legal divorce. If his divorce is invalid and he remarries, he is a bigamist. The sin rests on his shoulders, but not on his progeny's. Thus we have a double standard, as his former wife's children by her new husband are so branded. Even if on discovering that her divorce was illegal, she and her former husband go to an Orthodox *bet din* and obtain an

Orthodox divorce, her children are still accounted illegitimate. Any new children after the divorce are legal, but there is no *ex post facto* way to reclaim the once branded children, not by Orthodox law.

As of now this harsh interpretation of Jewish law by the Orthodox has caused relatively little personal hardship, because all divorce in Israel is in the hands of the traditional *bet din*. So every divorce in Israel, whether of the Orthodox or of the secular Jew, is according to Orthodox law. Outside Israel the Orthodox have neither plenary power nor a central registry to record all marriages and divorces as they do in Israel. So there are few examples of marriages refused or persons snubbed because of divorce in their background. When an American Jew wishes to marry an Israeli Jew in Israel, even though both may lean toward Liberal Judaism, they will have to supply an extensive record of family background to the Orthodox rabbis before they are given permission to be united.

An inkling of what may happen in the future may be supplied by the example of the Jews of India who migrated to Israel soon after the state was established. Though strictly traditional, their laws of divorce were different in some degree from that of the mainstream of Jewry because of the many centuries in which they were cut off from it. Faced with these minor divergences the Israeli rabbinate decreed that before any Indian Jew could marry a non-Indian Jew, his or her family tree had to be studied to see if there had been any divorce. If there had been any, marriage to a non-Indian Jew was prohibited. Marriage to a fellow Indian Jew was permitted, as that had been going on for centuries. Needless to say, the Indian Jews were incensed.

Liberal Jews in Israel have been trying, though so far without success, to remedy this situation and redo the laws of divorce so that a woman will be able to institute a divorce action and so that civil divorces from other lands will be recognized.

There is nothing in Jewish law or custom to deny the re-marriage of divorced mates to each other. According to the Orthodox such marriages may take place when other marriages are forbidden, such as on the *chol ha-moed,* the intermediary days of the festivals. But what of couples who were divorced and one of them married another mate? Now, after the dissolution of that second marriage, the first couple wish to remarry. May they? According to Orthodox sources, this would not be allowed (Deuteronomy 24:1–4). The reason was to discourage unthinking divorce and remarriage. However, modern Reform rabbis will usually perform such a marriage, especially if there are children of the first marriage involved. (See Solomon Freehof, *Recent Reform Responsa,* pp. 163–167.)

Just as a *kohen,* a descendant of the priestly class, may not marry a convert, so he may not marry a divorcee, not even his own former wife. Supposedly this was to protect priestly purity, and these restrictions are kept by the Orthodox for they maintain their hope that the Temple will be restored and the priests resume their cultic duties. This means that in Israel modern *kohanim* cannot marry a convert or divorcee, not even if they wish to relinquish their ties to the priestly caste and forgo a role in messianic days. If they insist on so marrying, they must go to Cyprus for a civil ceremony, which is recognized by the state at their return—but not by the rabbinate.

As Liberal Judaism does not hope for a restoration of the Temple sacrifices nor for any special cultic role for the *kohen,* it does not consider itself bound by these restrictions.

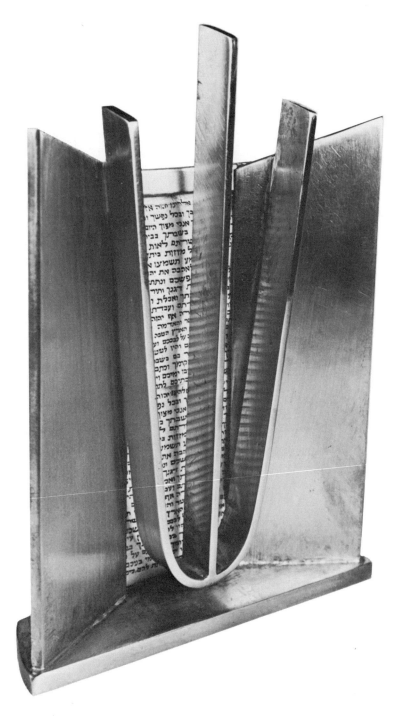

Shin for Shaddai

The Home

"Your tent is in peace" refers to the man who loves his wife as himself and honors her more than himself and who leads his children in the right path.

YEVAMOT 62b

Many are the Jewish items in the traditional home, expressions of physical as well as spiritual beauty: the *mezuzah, kiddush* goblets, Shabbat candlesticks, a *havdalah* set (a turreted spice box and a holder for the braided candle), a *Chanukah menorah,* perhaps a chased case for the *etrog,* a *seder* plate, an embroidered cover for the Shabbat *chalah,* as well as a special knife with engraved handle for the *chalah.*

A Jewish home can be recognized easily by the number of books: prayer books, the Holy Scriptures with their commentaries, *Haggadot,* frequently a set of the Talmud in ponderous volumes, history books, books of ethics and philosophy.

On the walls are found pictures of Jewish content, of Israel and its holy places, of Jewish dignitaries. There may be also a framed, intricately worked *mizrach* on the eastern wall, a hand-lettered page that shows the direction of Jerusalem, so that worshipers at home-devotions can know the correct way to face.

Certainly, Liberal Jews should include many of these in their homes. The ceremonial objects in reverent use, books and magazines, pictures and phonograph records, all con-

73

tribute to the sustenance of the Jewish mind as well as the furnishing of the Jewish home.

The Mezuzah

A *mezuzah* is affixed to the right entrance doorpost at eye level. The *mezuzah* case, usually of olive wood or metal, has a tiny aperture with the letter *shin* visible within, standing for the name *Shaddai,* the Almighty. Inside the case is a small parchment scroll, hand-inscribed with the *Shema,* "Hear, O Israel," and the paragraphs that follow, "Thou shalt love the Lord, thy God" (Deuteronomy 6:4–9; 11:13–21).

The *mezuzah* is put in a slanting position, the upper end pointing inward, the lower outward. This slanting position is the result of a difference between Rashi, the medieval French sage, and his grandson, Rabbenu Tam (Rabbi Jacob ben Meir). Rashi said that the *mezuzah* should be affixed vertically; Rabbenu Tam, horizontally. As a compromise, it is placed at a slant.

Maimonides, the great Jewish philosopher, said that the purpose of the *mezuzah* is to keep us constantly aware of God's divinity and of the moral duties of being a Jew (*Yad ha-Hazakah, Mezuzah* 5:5).

Traditional Jews on entering the house or leaving it, touch the *mezuzah* with their fingers and then kiss the fingers.

The origin of the *mezuzah* is in the "Thou shalt love" paragraph: "and thou shalt write them on the doorposts of thy house!" Originally, these words were actually written on the doorposts, but the wind and rain slowly effaced them. To prevent the defacing of the name of God, the rabbis prescribed the parchment scroll within the protective covering.

Most Liberal Jews place the *mezuzah* on their outside doorpost. Some may have it within, at the entrance, especially if the *mezuzah* is so finely wrought it cannot withstand the weather. There are strikingly beautiful, hand-made cases crafted here and in Israel. Certainly every Liberal Jew should have this ancient symbol of blessing at his door. Traditional Jews fix a *mezuzah* to the entrance of every regular room of the house, which would not include the kitchen, pantry or bathrooms.

Phylacteries

There are a number of ceremonial items of personal use that all Orthodox Jews hold important. The phylacteries, or *tefilin,* are used by all male traditional Jews over the age of Bar Mitzvah. The *tefilin* are two small leather boxes mounted on long leather straps. Like the *mezuzah,* they contain passages from the Torah, written on parchment by hand (Exodus 13:1–10, 11–16; Deuteronomy 6:4–9, 11:13–21). These biblical passages stress the duty of loving and serving God and observing the *mitzvot.* Like the *mezuzah,* they are supposed to be examined periodically to be sure that the writing has not faded.

One of the *tefilin* is worn on the forehead, its straps falling before either shoulder. The other is worn on the left arm, its box facing the heart. The strap is twined seven times around the arm, and it forms the letter *shin* for *Shaddai,* the Almighty, on the hand. The *tefilin* are donned at every weekday morning service by traditional Jews. Some continue to wear them after services while they study.

There are two types of *tefilin,* the so-called Rashi *tefilin* and those of Rabbenu Tam, the two medieval luminaries. They differ as to the order of the biblical quotations. There are even some ultra-Orthodox Jews who wear both sets of *tefilin* at prayer, lest they offend the memory of either of these two sages.

Not many Reform Jews wear phylacteries with any regularity. Orthodox Jews say that phylacteries are commanded in the "Thou shalt love" paragraph (Deuteronomy 6:8). Liberal

Jews say that this is figurative, that we remember with heart and mind. In proof of this we point to another passage in the Torah in which we are told to wear the Exodus from Egypt as a frontlet (Exodus 13:16).

Yarmulka

The *yarmulka* or *kipah* or *kapel* is a skullcap, and it has become a symbol of Judaism to many Jews. *Yarmulka* is a Slavic word; *kapel* is from the Italian *capello* or hat; *kipah* is Hebrew. To the traditional Jew today, praying or eating or mentioning the name of God without a head-covering would be regarded as blasphemous. Yet nowhere is this enjoined in Scripture or the Talmud. From talmudic statements it is clear that the sages did not appear in public without covering their heads (*Shabbat* 118b; *Kiddushin* 31a). However, the great mass of men of Israel did, and there is no connection made in these sources with a covered head and worship. The root of the idea of the sages covering their heads is more likely due to the Levantine idea of propriety, the man of dignity is always clad in proper garb, including head-covering.

Today the ultra-Orthodox wear a hat all day long, and even fall asleep at night with their *yarmulka* in place. When they go outside, their hat is placed over the *yarmulka*. Yet it is not difficult to show that only a few centuries ago traditional Jews worshiped with no thought of hat. Disquisitions have been written on the history and need of the *yarmulka,* yet they depend on circumstantial evidence to maintain their argument.

As it seems that the origin of the *kipah* is in the way the Eastern man showed reverence, so Liberal Judaism thought it only correct that as Western man shows reverence by removing his head-covering, he would do so. In early Reform all men worshiped bare-headed. Today, in many Reform congregations, the rabbi and cantor do wear the *kipah*. There are two reasons for this. One is that many members feel that this brings the precentors more in line with Jewish tradition, which has emphasized a head-covering. The other is that in the ancient Temple in Jerusalem, the officiating priests wore a headdress (Exodus 28:37-39). However, many congregations refuse this reasoning, saying that the rabbi and cantor have no sacerdotal function, and are not to be compared with the priests of yore in any way. There are some congregations which ask anyone who takes part in the service on the *bimah* to wear a *kipah.* In others it is not required, and in many it is interdicted entirely.

In many congregations the male worshiper may or may not wear a *kipah,* as he himself chooses. There are a few where he will be asked to remove his hat if he wears one. There are some where he will be asked to remove his street hat and substitute a *kipah,* but this is for esthetic reasons. And there are Reform congregations where every male wears a *kipah.*

The reason Orthodox Jews will always wear a hat when they eat is because they pronounce a prayer before and after the meal, and so must be covered. Also, there is the statement that when men eat together in amity and discuss words of Torah, God's Heavenly Spirit rests upon them (*Pirke Avot* 3:4).

An interesting point may be made in the defense of those Reform Jews who do not wear a *kipah.* The *Shulchan Aruch,* the ritual guide of Orthodox Jews, states that every male must wear a belt at prayer, to separate the holy from the profane, but it does not mention a hat. Yet visitors to Reform synagogs never inquire whether we wear a belt, but often whether we do wear hats at our services.

A number of Liberal congregations request that a woman wear a hat at services. Orthodox custom demands that a married woman cover her hair in the synagog. (Most Orthodox women will cover their hair whenever they are outside their own homes, not only in the synagog.) The unmarried woman will be hatless. However, the reasoning behind the Liberal congregations' request seems not to be based nearly as much on religious tradition as it is on Emily Post.

The Talit

Unlike the *kipah,* the wearing of the *talit* is enjoined in Scripture. In the book of Numbers (15:38,39), we read that the Israelites were commanded to wear a garment with fringes. The fringes at first were to include a thread of blue. The dye was derived from a Phoenician mollusk. When this dye became rare the rabbis allowed this part of the command to become inoperative.

The biblical passage states that the Israelites were to wear fringes "because I am the Lord who brought you out of the land of Egypt." At first glance this seems to be a non-sequitur. What have fringes to do with Egyptian slavery? The answer is that slaves of the time wore short robes so that they could be up and doing at the call of their master. A free man, especially in his leisure time, wore a long robe decorated with fringes. When the Israelites prayed, they did so as free men. The fringes, *tzitzit,* were to serve to remind them of their ancient slavery, when they could not wear a free man's robe. The stripes were added for beauty. A mystical meaning was soon added to the combination of knots in the fringes.

When the Jews no longer wore a robe as their regular garment, the fringed garment became a shawl thrown over the shoulders or covering the entire back as a prayer garment. Among the Sephardim, the Jews of the Iberian peninsula, a boy began such regular use at his Bar Mitzvah. Among the Ashkenazim, the Jews of central and eastern Europe, a young man would not wear one until he was married—the *talit* being a principal gift of the father of the bride to his new son-in-law. The *talit* is worn at morning prayers by the traditional Jew, in his home or in the synagog.

Liberal Jews for the most part dropped the wearing of the *talit*. They felt free without an additional garment. In many congregations today, however, the rabbi and cantor wear a *talit*, or the Reform *atarah*, a streamlined version. This is to perpetuate the old custom, and is a direct reminder that the priests in the Temple wore a special garb when officiating. Some Reform Jews do not like this reasoning for they aver that rabbi and cantor play no sacerdotal role.

Arba Kanfot

Orthodox Jewish males also wear a *talit katan* or *arba kanfot* beneath their garments all day long. This is a rectangular cotton cloth with a hole cut out for their head, and with fringes at each corner. It is to satisfy the biblical command to wear a fringed garment. Among the ultra-pious, the ends of the fringes are visible, hanging free. Despite the fact that he wears a *talit katan*, the traditional Jew also wears a regular *talit* when he prays. Not many Reform Jews wear a *talit katan*.

Kashrut

If three eat at a table and speak there words of the Torah, it is as if they have eaten at the altar of God.

Pirke Avot 3:4

A rabbi once began his book with the statement, "Reform Jews eat ham." A Texas congregation once ruled that a member who kept a *kosher* home (or belonged to a Zionist organization) would not have full voting rights. Such actions only show the passions that once were raised in the Liberal Jewish movement, passions which look inane today.

Many Reform Jews do eat ham; many do not. There are Reform rabbis who do not object to shrimp or spareribs, others whose diet at home or abroad is *glatt kosher,* absolutely in accord with the *kashrut* of traditional Judaism. And there are many who vary: some who have *kosher* homes but eat less discriminatingly outside their homes.

The Bible is explicit in its food restrictions: No carrion, or flesh of beasts killed by animals or that died from disease. It permits only beasts with cloven hoof and that chew the cud; or fish with fins and scales; or barnyard fowl. The early rabbis "put a fence" around these restrictions and added the need for *kosher* slaughter—lest there be undue cruelty or the beast not

81

A tree of life to those who cling to it

be healthy, as *kosher* slaughter includes careful inspection. Deriving their reasoning from the admonition not "to seethe a kid in its mother's milk" (Exodus 23:19), the rabbis added restrictions against eating milk products and meat together, or even mixing utensils used for one or the other. Further restrictions were added through the ages until the standard *lamehadrin,* "for the glorifiers," was reached. This concept of superlative *kashrut* arose because the Orthodox maintain that he who exceeds a biblical or talmudic ordinance reaps an additional *mitzvah.* Thus the strict observance of *kashrut* led to many Orthodox rabbis spending much of their communal time deciding whether a chicken was *kosher* or not because of a spot on its liver or lungs. Though this may have meant that a poor person did without his hard-earned Sabbath meal, it also protected the health of the Jewish community in days before government inspection of meat.

The idea that *kosher* laws really are health rules is a point often made by apologists. This reasoning however misses the central point. There is no denying that swine harbor the dire disease trichinosis, that shellfish can be swarming with harmful germs and neither by smell nor taste demonstrate their lethal qualities. The chances of contracting a fell disease from beef or pike are slight.

Yet, if you were to say to a traditional Jew that the laws of *kashrut* are health rules, he would deny it. He is not surprised to discover that the Bible's injunctions are conducive to health; he would be astounded to hear that they were injurious. His obeying has nothing to do with health. He is observing the *mitzvot,* God's commands.

Conservative rabbis have often said that there is a spiritual and ethical lesson in *kashrut.* As one learns to curb his appetite for forbidden foods, even though they be tasty and not harmful, so one learns to curb his appetite in all areas of life, to learn to live moderately and purely. And traditional rabbis warn, "Do not say I will not eat ham because I hate it. Though it be sweet to you, do not eat it because it is forbidden."

Liberal Judaism does not prescribe *kashrut,* neither does it condemn it. The guiding criterion is internal: whatever is meaningful to you, either spiritually, or as a link with the past, or with the whole house of Israel, by all means do! If *kosher* or partially *kosher* seems a true sign of a Jewish home, it is most important that the home be kept that way.

Many Liberal rabbis and laymen observe "biblical *kashrut,*" but not talmudic: they do not eat the flesh of animals or fish prohibited by the Torah. But they do not insist on the complete separation of *milchig* and *fleishig,* milk and meat and the silverware and utensils for milk and meat, as ordained in the Talmud.

Each Liberal Jew must decide his own relationship to *kashrut.* Many Reform Jews consider *kashrut* peripheral to Judaism. If so, Liberal Judaism causes them no difficulty. If you do not think that *kashrut* will add to the meaning of your experience as a Jew, you will find no problem confronting you as a Reform Jew. But please be aware that every Reform synagog contains many who disagree, and find meaningful satisfaction in the complete or partial observance of an age-old Jewish custom.

Family Purity

When Orthodox Jews speak of family purity they are not merely referring to discouragement of marrying outside the Jewish fold. They are speaking of *taharat ha-mishpachah,* which connotes the relationships of husband and wife, the woman's cleanliness and uncleanliness, the use of the *mikveh,* or ritual bath, the ban on double beds, the connubial duties owed by husband to wife and wife to husband, etc.

The insistence on ritual purity of the married couple, and the woman in particular, has always been of major importance in Judaism, and unquestionably was of significance in preserving the health of the Jewish people.

Bathing in a *mikveh,* which consisted of first washing well and then entering a bath of running water, meant that each male bathed at least on the eve of the Sabbath and holy days, and each woman at least once a month. The woman was forbidden to her husband during her period and for seven days thereafter. Then she would go to the *mikveh* to bathe. Physicians agree that this was a most salutary health law. Of course, to the Orthodox these were not merely health laws but ways of godliness.

Reform Judaism maintains that cleanliness is easily assured in modern times and regards the use of the *mikveh* as a personal decision.

Shaatnez

Shaatnez is a mixture of wool and linen and is prohibited in the Torah (Leviticus 19:19), along with other mixtures such as sowing combinations of seeds or the mating of diverse animals. Even yoking diverse animals together is forbidden. Orthodox Jews will not use diverse wools together, such as a mixture of lamb's wool and goat's wool or of wool sewn with a linen thread.

One might ask whether we may use fruits that are the result of graftings. Dr. Solomon Freehof points out that even Orthodox Jews use *etrogim,* citrons, which are the product of citron grafts on the stronger lemon trees, so grafting is obviously permissible to any Jew (*Recent Reform Responsa,* p. 221).

Orthodox Jews examine all their new garments carefully to be sure that there is no admixture. As even Rashi cannot find any reason for this ban, Reform Jews do not observe it.

Orthodox Jews also leave a small portion of any garment unfinished just as they always leave a small portion of a house unpainted. These are signs of mourning for the destruction of the Temple.

Shaving

Many Orthodox men do not shave at all, though some will use a depilatory or, strange to relate, an electric shaver. The reasoning behind this is rather devious. The Torah says, "You shall not round the corners of your heads, nor mar the corners of your beard" (Leviticus 19:27). This is why Orthodox Jews leave the *peot,* sidecurls, even though they may crop the rest of the head. The original law against shaving with a razor is for the Nazirite (Numbers 6:5). Later it was taken to mean any Jew's use of a razor (*Numbers Rabah* 10:10). Other means of removing face hair were condoned (*Mishnah Makot* 3:5).

The chemical depilatory therefore is considered permissible. The electric razor passes muster as there is a shield or a screen between the moving blade and the face, so there is a presumption that the blade does not touch the face, or it is considered a kind of electric scissors, which are permitted.

Reform Jews do not obey this ban on shaving with a razor, nor do they insist on subterfuges. We know from the Jerusalem Talmud (*Rosh Hahanah,* I, law 3) that the Jews of ancient days did shave and it was not considered a sin at all.

Heal us, O Lord, and we shall be healed

Illness

Poverty and sickness are easier to bear with faith.
IBN GABIROL, MIVHAR HA-PENINIM

In primitive societies people thought that sickness was caused by demons. Early Jewish sources provide examples of curing by driving out evil spirits. There is no question that most people were convinced that spirits and demons worked their will on man. It is only recently that the making and selling of amulets are no longer prevalent among Jews. Oriental Jews still use them and they can be purchased, either for curio value or for actual use, in many shops.

Brass hands inscribed with the prescribed words are used to fend off the evil eye. Amulets written on parchment or paper are hung about a mother-to-be's bed or a baby's cradle, to ward off Lilith, Adam's first wife, whose jealousy causes her to steal babies.

Though the ignorant and superstitious fought off demons, the teachers of Judaism taught disease must be fought by other means. They recommended prayer to God as well as the development and full use of medical science.

Judaism rejects the idea that man must submit to illness as God's will and therefore accept it with resignation and not try to conquer it. On the contrary, Judaism teaches that man is

87

God's assistant in preserving human life, and that a Jew fulfills God's will when he makes use of a physician and medicine. So even in early days Jewish physicians became skilled. From the Middle Ages to the present Jewish physicians can be numbered among the foremost of their craft: Maimonides and Judah Halevi are only some of the great Jews in medicine. The synagog was never as restrictive of medical research or other practices as was the church.

However, even today we find people who blame illness on God—"Why did this have to happen to me? What did I do that God should let this happen?" One can sympathize with such plaints even as we reject them, for they arise from the pain and weakness of illness. Judaism says that it is our duty to direct our hearts to God, to pray for strength and recovery. If we consider our past misdeeds—and a bed of pain is often an occasion for long meditation—it should be to resolve to live in such a way as to be worthy of God's gift of life.

Therefore Judaism avers that every action that helps us to be healthful is desirable, from obtaining the best physician to desisting from habits that shorten or endanger life. Nor are we allowed to turn to faith-healing cults, which misuse the teachings of religion and dispense with the science of medicine. Prayer may cause miracles—any physician, any rabbi, can attest to this from personal experience—but one may not depend on miraculous intervention. We cannot know why a prayer does help in one instance, and have no effect in another. We do know why medicine will help in most instances. The two together are far better than only one.

The Preservation of Life

The preservation of life, *pikuach nefesh,* has always been a cardinal rule of Judaism. Such dilemmas as occur within the Roman Catholic faith, where a woman is in grave danger in childbirth, and the doctors can save either the mother or the child, do not exist in Judaism. The life of the mother must take precedence. She exists, therefore she has her right to life; the unborn foetus is not yet truly alive. The unborn must give way to the living.

So, too, every *mitzvah* must give way to the need to save a life. Even the most Orthodox will permit an ambulance to take a stricken person to a hospital or a surgeon to perform an emergency operation on the Sabbath.

Even the most Orthodox will permit eating on Yom Kippur for a sick person, lighting a fire on the Sabbath to keep him warm, or any other infringement of law or custom to preserve life. The great Salanter, Rabbi Israel Lipkin, when his city was threatened by plague, hearkened to the advice of the town physicians that no one fast on Yom Kippur lest his strength to resist be diminished. The rabbi not only ordered all the Jews to eat on that day of the White Fast, he himself and two other rabbis ascended the *bimah*, in full sight of the congregation. They each ate a roll after reciting the benediction, lest anyone think that the rabbis considered themselves above the rules they set for the layman.

The saving of life is an imperative in Judaism. A person who smokes or drinks to excess or takes drugs undermines his own health and is considered one who commits suicide in stages, and the suicide is abhorred as one who denies life given by God.

This reverence for life goes so far that if a woman with child wishes to eat that which is ordinarily forbidden, non-*kosher* food, the Talmud itself gives permission for her to do so, lest she and the child within her be affected (*Yoma* 82a).

Visiting the Sick

For hundreds of years there existed *Bikur Cholim* societies, groups of laymen who visited and cared for the sick. Before hospitals and nurses' care, such groups were imperative. The visiting of the sick, even if only to express one's sympathies, has always been a *mitzvah*. "He who does not visit the sick is like a murderer," said Rabbi Akiba (*Nedarim* 40a). Even today, when hospitals and nurses do exist, and we depend on their professional care, concern for the sick and visiting them are necessary. Often the psychological benefit of a friendly visit can aid a patient's recovery.

It is the custom for one who has recovered from a serious illness or escaped from a great danger to recite the *Gomel* prayer, *shegemalani kol tov,* "who has saved me from all evil," or "who has favored me with all good." So, too, it is customary to give to charity.

Prolonged Illness

Judaism is a realistic religion. Though it is basically a religion of hope, yet must we learn to face prolonged illness and death. The person who is ill for a long time, especially if there seems little chance of recovery, sometimes is difficult to himself and to the people around him. Giving the patient courage, preserving our own courage, these are necessities. Judaism says that we must never give up hope, yet it recognizes the seriousness of such a situation, and does not make light of it. The will to life, the respect for the person, the preservation of personality, the need for faith in God, the God of life and of death, these are our guidelines. Prayer and meditation are our spiritual armor, based on our faith in a deathless God.

Euthanasia

When there is pain the doctor's case of drugs must be used in its entirety. However, euthanasia (mercy-killing) is not to be countenanced, even in cases of extreme pain. Murder is yet murder. However, this does not mean that the physician or family must preserve any semblance of life at any cost, whether of dignity or of money when life is surely ebbing away. The addition of a day or even a week of coma or of pain is unnecessary and an affront to the meaning of life. Not that death should be induced, but it can be allowed to come when it wills.

Changing the Name

There is an old superstition of changing the name of a seriously ill person. It arose from the hope of fooling the angel of death. Often a sick man was renamed Chayim, or a woman Chavah, each of which means life, trusting that the new name would be prophetic and help restore the patient to life. It has no place in Liberal Judaism.

Final Rite

There is no deathbed sacrament in Judaism. Certainly we do not feel that God would be displeased if we do not send for a rabbi or recite prescribed words at the final hour. Yet there is a Jewish tradition of *vidui,* of a statement of confession as the end approaches. This may be simply the recital of the *Shema* as an affirmation of faith, or it may be the traditional Prayer for the Dying (see Glossary or *Rabbi's Manual,* pp. 59–62).

The rabbi should be informed, for he will want to be with the family as the end approaches and certainly after the death. The actual passing is greeted with the words *Baruch Dayan ha-emet,* "Blessed is the righteous Judge," a basic expression of faith at the hour of loss.

The Funeral

Death is inevitable. The sadness, the sense of irremediable, ineffable loss can only be mitigated by the teachings of our religion and the solicitude of friends. Faith and love are the only real specifics at such a time.

The principal purposes of the funeral are to bury the body of the deceased with proper dignity, and to provide comfort for the bereaved. The Jewish religious funeral service is meant to present an understanding of God and His ways, of our life and our mortality, so as to enable the mourner to accept his own deep feelings. Jewish tradition deals with death realistically, with a sense of finality. It is at the same time concerned with life as well as death, both of which are viewed in the light of eternity.

It has been the Jewish custom not to delay the funeral, burial taking place within twenty-four hours. This was probably due to two reasons. The Jews lived in a semi-tropical country and refused to use any form of embalming. So it was expedient to conduct the burial as soon as possible. This habit was retained even when Jews lived in more temperate climes. The second reason is even more pertinent today. It was recognized that the principal grief occurs while the body is yet un-

93

buried, while it lies before the mourners. The rabbis realized that in this greatest grief, the family could not be expected to carry on even the religious duties of mourners, let alone their usual familial and other duties. The finality of the burial marked an end to this period of nothingness, a period where even the visits of close friends were discouraged. After the burial came the period of *shivah,* of regular mourning, of visits and prayer services in the home.

A problem that arises more often today than formerly has to do with the coming of the Sabbath before the dead are buried. Formerly, the funeral was held even with a few hours' preparation, so that rarely was a burial held over from Friday until Sunday morning. But today this does happen as there are many more preparations necessary.

When this happened in earlier days, the mourners were considered to be free from attending all services until the actual interment, including the Sabbath services. Liberal Jewish families may want to attend services, for the consolations of our religion are great. Not all rabbis are agreed as to whether they may. Dr. Israel Bettan said they may and *Kaddish* may be recited for the deceased, even though they are unburied. Rabbi Solomon Freehof said the family should not attend and *Kaddish* may not be recited for the deceased unless there is an overriding reason. All would agree that this would be contrary to usual Orthodox custom, but Dr. Freehof in Volume II of his *Reform Jewish Practice,* page 120, quotes David ben Samuel Halevi, "If a death occurs on the Sabbath or holidays when burial cannot take place, the *Kaddish* should be said immediately after the *death,* for the saying of *Kaddish* is not dependent on the beginning of the period of mourning."

Embalming and Autopsy

Embalming is prohibited by Orthodox Jews. It is considered an insult to the dead to do more than clean the body for burial. As the body is to return to the earth, embalming interferes with natural processes. Reform Judaism permits embalming for any good reason, as the body will return to the dust of which it is made sooner or later.

So, too, traditional Jews are against autopsy, except when it can clearly be shown that such a medical procedure will have a beneficial effect on the living. Even today the Orthodox will refuse to allow autopsy unless the death was caused by a disease which is under immediate study, where the pathologist's report has a good likelihood of effecting a breakthrough in the study of the disease. An autopsy just for the hospital's statistics is not countenanced by the Orthodox.

Liberal Jews agree that the disfigurement of the body of a beloved one for exiguous reasons should not be permitted. But just as Liberal Judaism permits embalming, if there is reason for it, so it permits autopsy if there is reason. In many instances the rabbi will be on the physician's side in urging the family to acquiesce to this seeking for cause and remedy. Allowing the eyes or other organs of the deceased to be removed so that they can be transplanted to a living person is entirely in accord with the tenets of Judaism. This is not an act of mutilation, which is forbidden, but an act of healing and help.

Before the Funeral

Liberal Jews will at times delay a funeral a day or even two for exigent reasons. But the force of tradition should not lightly be dispensed with, for there is no denying the psychological help of immediate burial. The finality of burial marks the end of the first period, the private period, of mourning. Lengthening this period or tampering with it, so that the mourners are expected to receive friends before the burial, are serious mistakes which bring additional stress and pain.

Recently some people have begun to emulate non-Jews and hold a visiting session at the home or the funeral parlor the evening before the funeral. This is for the convenience of the friends and provides only anguish to the mourners. It is a dreadful innovation. It is also used as a time for public viewing of the corpse, a grisly idea and repugnant to Judaism. The members of the immediate family may have a private last look at their beloved. The public has no need to view a cosmetic-daubed version of the deceased. All branches of Judaism agree that the coffin should be closed firmly at the funeral.

Orthodox Jews keep watchers sitting at the bier of the deceased the night before the burial. Usually the watcher will recite psalms during his vigil. As the reason for the watcher is based on superstitious fear of the depradations of spirits or fear that animals may get to the body, with modern funeral establishments we may dispense with such precautions.

Candles are usually lit in the room with the deceased. This has a symbolic meaning, that the quenched light of life continues in the remembrance of the living—and within the spirit of God. So Liberal Jews will usually have such candles lit.

Cremation

Cremation is completely banned by traditional Jews for religious reasons. Only in a time of plague might it be permitted. Orthodox Jews believe in a bodily resurrection at the "end of days." When this takes place, the bodies of the once dead are supposed to come together and be renewed. If the ashes have been spread, the soul will have trouble reclaiming its body. Liberal Jews do permit cremation. The ashes should be placed in an urn and buried with proper ritual in a Jewish cemetery or placed in a proper vault.

Cemetery

All burial should be in a Jewish cemetery, though it may take place in a non-sectarian cemetery which is not markedly of another faith, and a Jewish marker should be placed over the grave. Jewish interment was usually burial, but we know that two thousand years ago the rabbis of the *Sanhedrin* were laid to rest on the shelves of underground crypts. Therefore we cannot say that mausoleums are not in consonance with Jewish tradition, even though they do not answer the logic of the phrase, "The dust is returned to the earth from which it came."

Coffins

The use of concrete burial vaults to contain the coffin or elaborate caskets is foreign to traditional Judaism. There are two reasons. Metal caskets and vaults are used to prevent the deterioration of the body, and this is a denial of the reality and the finality of the experience of death. The second reason is that we hold that all are equal in death, rich and poor, learned and simple. Therefore any rich display is invidious and out of place at such a time.

Traditional Jews do not allow any flowers at a funeral. They say that the cut life of the dead is only mocked by the brief beauty of the cut flowers. While some Liberal Jews allow the judicious use of flowers, formal expressions of friends' sympathy may better be directed to memorial funds, the temple, or to other benevolent interests of the deceased.

In most Jewish communities the dead were all buried in simple pine coffins, made without nails or any metal at all. In Jerusalem the dead have always been buried in their shrouds, without any coffin. Reform Jews do not insist on such simplicity, but expensive and ornate caskets are foreign to all branches of Judaism. So is any form of ostentation. Simplicity and dignity are the manifestations of reverence for the dead.

The Clothing

Traditional Jews are buried wearing *tachrichim,* simple white burial garments. Men wear their *talit* and a *yarmulka.* The body is cleansed according to the strict detailed instructions of the *Shulchan Aruch*. A small sack of earth from Israel is placed under the head to assist the dead to rise, as the resurrection will take place in the land of Israel. Sometimes shards are placed over the eyes, as a symbol that the eyes have now ceased their searching. Reform Jews do not use the sack of earth or the shards, and assuredly not the coins which some people place over the eyes, as these are derived from the ferry-fare for Charon to cross the river Styx, of ancient Greek mythology. The body should be clad in a suit or dress that was part of the regular wardrobe. The *talit* may be worn, if that is customary in the synagog to which the deceased belonged.

Planning the Funeral

Preparations for funerals may be made on the afternoons of the Sabbath and festivals, and even Rosh Hashanah afternoon, to spare the family the anguish of delay, but not on Yom Kippur. Funerals may not be held on the Sabbath, festivals, or High Holy Days, except in time of plague, when public health demands.

The Funeral Service

The chapel funeral service is of recent origin. Originally there was a brief psalm service in the home, the cortege passed the synagog, whose door was opened in respect, and the major service was graveside. The difficulty in reaching distant cemeteries and the wish of large numbers to be present at at least part of the funeral produced the chapel service. Care must be taken that it is conducted entirely as the sober religious event it is.

Only the Jewish service should be held. The elaborate fraternal order services are compendia from ancient pagan and non-Jewish sources. They must not be held in any synagog. They should be discouraged anyplace, for their symbols are completely non-Jewish: a sprig of evergreen is pagan, an apron disrespectful. If insisted on, such services must take place separately, not as though part of the Jewish service.

Any informed Jewish male may conduct a Jewish funeral. However, it is disrespectful to have a funeral director conduct such a service except in an emergency.

It is a religious duty to attend a funeral of someone known to us, but not if a Jew is buried with non-Jewish rites, for that is insulting to Judaism. Apostates may be buried in a Jewish cemetery, even if they have not definitely returned to Judaism before their death. But their service and burial must entirely be Jewish.

Traditional Jews do not have music at a funeral. Reform Jews may want simple background music. Care should be taken that this be dignified and if supplied by non-Jews, not of distinctly non-Jewish character.

The Jewish custom has always been to hold funerals during the day, except in the most unusual circumstances. It was felt that a nighttime service was lacking in dignity. As until recently the major part of the service was graveside, a night funeral was inexpedient altogether. Reform Jews usually concur with this tradition, but a memorial service may be held at night.

Eulogies

The Jewish funeral service has contained a eulogy from time immemorial. However, no eulogies were delivered at certain periods of the year, the month of Nisan, for instance, or during the weeks of Pesach or Sukot. Supposedly the joy of

Israel in its holiday supervened. Modern traditional rabbis sometimes escape these regulations by delivering a brief eulogy while denying that they are doing so, as they recognize the weight such words of remembrance have in easing the grief of the mourners. Liberal Judaism does not concur with the idea of denying the deceased the eulogy they deserve, nor are any subterfuges necessary. Judaism does not allow fulsome praise or, conversely, speaking ill of the dead. If the deceased did not deserve praise, then the eulogy should speak of life and death, of faith and its power, and avoid recriminations.

It has long been the custom for those who have served the community well in positions of trust to be buried from the synagog. Some congregations limit this honor to clearly defined former holders of office. Other congregations, not wishing to select any member for such a dignity, say that the family of any member in good standing may so arrange.

Pallbearers

There is no basic objection to a Christian serving as pallbearer at a Jewish funeral. The Talmud requires that if a body must be buried on the first day of a holy day (because of a plague), Gentiles must attend to the burial (*Betza* 6a). Therefore, there is no question that they may assist in a normal burial.

As the bearing of the coffin is considered a great *mitzvah,* so great that Jews who do so are excused from the *mitzvah* of prayer that day, the honor should go to Jews. But if there are gentile friends who were particularly close to the deceased, they may be given this sad privilege.

Traditional Jews usually do not allow the children of the deceased to serve as pallbearers. There is no basis for this in law nor in more than local custom. So if any child wishes to, he should be allowed to assist.

A Jew may participate as a pallbearer at a gentile funeral. He may deliver the eulogy or act as a pallbearer.

The valley of the shadow

Liberal Practice

Many are the customs and practices of Orthodox Judaism concerning funerals that Reform Jews no longer observe:

The tearing of the garments, a traditional sign of mourning, largely has been supplanted by the snipping of a black ribbon affixed to the mourners' garments, and is not widely practiced by Reform Jews.

The lining up of those attending the interment so that the mourners can pass through their midst is not usual in Reform.

Nor does Reform Judaism insist that the grave be filled with earth within view of the mourners. This was done to emphasize the finality of death. Few of us need such emphasis.

Nor do we continue old superstitions such as throwing a handful of grass over the shoulder when leaving the cemetery, entering the home through a rear door, washing the hands at the entrance, or covering all mirrors or turning them to the wall, nor need a glass of water be set out for the soul to wash itself. Nor are the dead buried with sticks in their hands. These are superstitions and based on the belief in spirits.

The Suicide

Traditionally suicide was considered such a dreadful sin that there was no real service. The body was buried at the edge of the graveyard and there was no formal mourning.

However, the name for the suicide in Hebrew is *hamiaved atzmo bedaat,* "he who causes himself to be lost with knowledge." This points out the Jewish view, that a true suicide is a person who without any deranging illness or nervous condition takes his own life. This is extremely rare. Therefore Reform Jews will usually hold that a suicide is the victim of a severe trauma or illness that made balance of mind impossible. Accordingly, suicides are treated as any other person who died of an illness.

Reburial

If a body has been buried and later the family wishes to move the grave, this may be done if there is good reason. To do so frivolously is considered a desecration. To allow the whole family to rest together is considered a pertinent and valid reason.

Mourning

Woe to the losers, not to the lost.
He is at rest: it is we who mourn.
MOED KATAN 25b

Traditional Judaism has set exact rules to the mourning of a near relative. It realizes the need for catharsis. It is deeply aware of the need for communication and the danger of excessive introverted solitary meditation. It calls for the salutary visits of sympathetic friends who join in the religious practices as well, of services and ritual that combine the special meaning of the week of *shivah* with the regular Orthodox routine of thrice-daily prayer. Traditional Judaism intends this to deepen the religious consolation of faith, relate the mourner fully to the deceased *and* to the world about him, his relatives and friends, and to help him relink himself to the daily round.

Once the family returns to the home in which they will sit *shivah* (taken from the word *sheva,* seven, for it is a seven-day period of mourning), the prescribed routine fulfills psychological as well as religious and even social purposes. The family is together, for the immediate mourners may not leave the home until their week of mourning is done—except to go to the synagog on the Sabbath (the rest of the week the service comes to them), or in an emergency. This means that family

105

solidarity is underlined. It means that the survivors are drawn nearer to each other. They sit on boxes or on the ground, for they will not sit comfortably this week. They wear slippers to show they are going no place. The men do not cut their beards for thirty days. There is no music or any thought of entertainment. People are in and out, many bearing gifts of food, for the mourners are constrained from regular activity.

One of the most important reasons for this busyness is to reduce the opportunity of a mourner's brooding, with the usually unwarranted but frequent self-accusations of "I didn't do enough," or "I did not help when I should," natural reactions as a person tries to reconstruct the happenings of the last months or days, but invariably fruitless and often destructive. Being with relatives and friends, those who are closest and most dear, is the best palliative to this danger. We are admonished by the rabbis not to let conversation at such times be frivolous, as this is desecration, nor get morbid, as this is dangerous.

Liberal Mourning Practices

Reform Judaism while recognizing the religious, familial and psychological validity that underlies all these customs, has softened them. Mourners need not remain in the house to which they return after the funeral, but may go to their own homes afterwards. If they live near other members of the family they should sleep at home, but spend the day and evening together at the home of the eldest or at the largest home. If they do not live near each other, they should endeavor to spend at least the first three days together. This three-day period is recognized even by the Orthodox as the more rigorous part of the period. So if a person must attend to business, he is allowed to do so after the first three days. In Reform, either the seven- or the three-day period of mourning is acceptable. Usually Reform Jews sit on regular chairs, they do not wear slippers, and the men will shave. Services are held in the home on weekdays, led either by the rabbi or any informed layman, sometimes only the first day, more usually for three days, sometimes for the full week. The Reform service for a house of mourning or the regular Reform weekday service is used. For a Reform family suddenly to switch to Orthodox practices at mourning often leads to misunderstanding, and fails to provide the consolation that comes from the known, the accepted, the habitual.

A *minyan,* a quorum of ten men, is not imperative in Reform, but the presence of ten people is desirable. Most important, women are included. The Orthodox custom of the women leaving the room in which the men are praying is repugnant to Liberal Judaism. The women need the prayers as much as do the men.

The traditional seven-day candle is lit by all Jews after the return from the cemetery, though any special light will do.

Children may attend school after the first day or two; an adult may return to work after three days or the seven-day mourning period. A physician may attend the seriously ill on even the first day if only he can be of help.

If, because of distance or failure of communication, one learns of the death of an immediate member of the family after the burial has taken place, he should observe one day of mourning plus the restriction of social affairs and entertainment.

Traditional Jews abstain from entertainment and any form of music for a full year after the death of parents. Liberal Jews usually desist for the first thirty days. Attendance at civic or congregational functions (aside from the purely social) is permissible after *shivah* and during the thirty-day period. After the thirty days, the mourner will resume his normal social life, if he is ready to do so.

Tradition prohibits remarriage for at least ninety days after the death of a spouse. A widow with dependent children who needs the help of a provider may marry even before, but it is considered a *mitzvah* to help her so that she may wait the full ninety days.

It is important to note that traditional Jews do not mourn for an infant who died within thirty days of birth, for the thinking is that such a babe never developed into a real human being. There is burial but not a full burial service and no regular mourning. An infant over a month old who dies is treated as a real person with regular funeral and mourning.

Kaddish

The *Kaddish* is the prayer that is recited at the close of the service and is considered the mourners' prayer. It is not a prayer for the dead. The prayer that actually mentions the dead is the *El Male Rachamim,* "O Lord, Full of Mercies," which is recited at funerals and at *Yizkor,* memorial services (see Glossary for translations). The *Kaddish* too is recited at funerals and memorial services, but it is recited at every regular service as well. In traditional synagogs it is recited often, in varying forms, to mark the conclusion of different portions of the service. The final recitation is considered the "Mourners' *Kaddish.*"

Actually, there is no mention of mourning or the dead in the *Kaddish.* Its theme is the affirmation of life, of the greatness and holiness of God, of the quest for peace and holiness in our own lives and that of all Israel. It may be termed the Jewish doxology. The *Kaddish* was originally recited at the close of the study session in ancient days. It is in Aramaic, the language of the Talmud and the tongue used in daily conversation two thousand years ago. As study was considered a prime method to honor the memory of the dead, a study session of the Torah or a religious discourse was conducted for the mourners and closed with the prayer that usually closed such a session. Soon the prayer was recognized as the mourners' prayer. Its solemn declaration of faith proved to be precisely in accord with the Jewish reaction to death: affirmation of belief in God's reign.

There are a number of forms of the *Kaddish* in Orthodoxy. Especially different is the *Kaddish le-Ithadta,* which is recited at Orthodox funerals. The words which are added do mention death and seek compassion on the soul of the departed (see Glossary for translation). Many Reform rabbis do not use this special *Kaddish,* mainly because the mourners are asked to join in the recitation of the *Kaddish* at the graveside. Using this different and difficult form of the *Kaddish* which is unfamiliar to most worshipers, makes it impossible for them to join in its recitation, whereas the repetition of the familiar words acts as a consolation and a reinforcement in a moment of stress.

The Reform Version

The *Union Prayer Book* version of the *Kaddish* contains an extra paragraph (*al Yisrael veal tzadikaya,* "for Israel and for its pious ones"), which does include the mention of the dead. This paragraph which is not traditional was added in the early nineteenth century to the Hamburg Temple prayer book. The paragraph is not taken from the special funeral *Kaddish.* Some rabbis use it; some do not—those who do not prefer to keep the *Kaddish* a prayer of solemn affirmation. Those who use it think that it adds pertinence to the prayer.

The words in English printed on the opposite page of the *Kaddish* in the *Union Prayer Books* are more a paraphrase than an exact rendering. The original Hebrew is much stronger (see Glossary for exact translation).

The *El Male Rachamim* prayer as recited by Reform rabbis or chanted by Reform cantors has been shortened. Almost all leave out the line which details the contribution to charity which has been made by the mourners in honor of the deceased. Liberal Judaism would say that the charity should be remembered, but its announcement at such a time is not necessary. The version of this prayer in the *Rabbi's Manual* is truncated to eliminate any seeming anthropomorphism or description of an After-World. Some Reform rabbis may restore some of the dropped lines. Consult the Glossary for a translation that is complete except for the sentence concerning the charitable donation.

The Recitation

The *Kaddish* is recited by the immediate mourners—spouse, children, parents or siblings of the departed. Orthodox mourners recite the *Kaddish* at the close of each of the thrice-a-day services, preferably with a *minyan,* though they may pray alone. After the first *yahrzeit* (anniversary of the death), the *Kaddish* is recited by a mourner on *yahrzeits* and at *Yizkor* (memorial) prayers.

Orthodox Jews actually recite the *Kaddish* for their parents only for eleven months after the day of burial. According to Jewish tradition the souls of the dead are exposed to a kind of Purgatory to cleanse them from their sins, before they are admitted to *Gan Eden,* Paradise. Any cleansing which lasted more than a year would be considered punishment rather than cleansing. As only the real sinner needs cleansing for a full year, traditional Jews say *Kaddish* for only eleven months, lest it seem that they were implying that their loved one needed a full year's cleansing in atonement for his sins.

As this reason seems not in consonance with the spirit of Liberal Judaism, Reform Jews recite the *Kaddish* for a twelve-month.

Many Reform Jews recite the *Kaddish* daily for the year, either at the synagog or at home. Others recite it regularly only at the Sabbath services in the synagog. In most traditional synagogs only the mourners rise for the mourners' *Kaddish.* In many Liberal synagogs, all present rise as a congregation. This helps provide additional consolation for the mourners, does not separate them from the rest of the worshipers, and they are made to feel that everyone present is joining with them in their grief.

Liberal Jews usually do not take three steps backward when finishing the *Kaddish,* as do the Orthodox, if only because of the fixed seating of our synagogs. Supposedly, this was to show that the worshiper was backing away from the presence of the King of Kings.

Traditional Jews do not recite *Kaddish* for Gentiles, but Liberal Jews may if they so desire.

Visiting the Grave

Traditional Jews do not visit the graves of their departed until the *sheloshim,* the one-month mourning period, is over. Liberal Jews may visit after the *shivah* period. One does not visit graves on a Sabbath or festivals, nor are public memorials held on these days. It is traditional to visit the graves of parents in the month before Rosh Hashanah, and many people do so on the *yahrzeit* day itself.

When one visits a grave it is traditional to recite the *Kaddish* prayer. On a *yahrzeit* the *El Male Rachamim* may also be recited. One does not need a rabbi or other religious functionary to recite these prayers. Anyone may do so. If one cannot read Hebrew, the words may be found transliterated in the *Union Prayer Book,* I (page 78) or one may read the English words (see Glossary). Even in Orthodox Judaism, a prayer in any language understood by the reciter is in order.

The Monument

Traditional Jews set up a monument which is unveiled at the close of the eleventh month. The elaborate Unveiling of the Monument service, which has sprung up as a kind of second funeral, sometimes replete with an additional eulogy, is of very recent origin. The usual unveiling was a private, brief ceremony for the immediate family alone. Any Jew who can recite the *El Male Rachamim* and the *Kaddish* can officiate (*Union Prayer Book,* Vol. I, p. 385; *Union Home Prayer Book,* p. 36).

The monument itself may be of stone or of metal. It may stand or lie flat. Ostentation should not be encouraged. The monument should include the name of the deceased in Hebrew as well as in English.

Yahrzeit

The word *yahrzeit* is from the German and means "year's time." It marks the anniversary of the death of a close relative. Traditional Jews observe the *yahrzeit* in accordance with the Hebrew calendar. Many Reform Jews use the secular calendar. The day of *yahrzeit* begins with sundown on the day before and continues for twenty-four hours. A candle or other special light should be lit. If the congregation does not have a daily service, the mourner should attend at the Sabbath service immediately following.

Most congregations read the names of the deceased whose *yahrzeits* occur during that week. This is not imperative, and a mourner will recall his own dear one during the recitation of the *Kaddish,* whether the name is read or not. Having the name read and not being present for no important reason is an insult to the memory of the deceased. If one cannot be present for an exigent reason, one should request the rabbi not to read the name and recite the *Kaddish* in privacy.

Orthodox Jews fast on the *yahrzeit* of a parent and repent for their sins. They do so that their atonement may obtain Divine Grace for the dead. Liberal Jews should not schedule social functions on that day. It is customary to give to charity in memory of the deceased on his *yahrzeit*.

Yizkor

Yizkor, remember, is the initial word of the prescribed prayer of the *Hazkarat Neshamot,* the Memorial Service. The word *yizkor* has become the title of this service for most people. Originally it was confined to the Day of Atonement. Since the eighteenth century, this service has been added to the Orthodox morning service of the last day of Pesach, the second day of Shavuot and the eighth day of Sukot or Shemini Atzeret.

The *Yizkor* service has become both more and less important in Liberal Judasim. The service itself has been lengthened to give due stress to this emotional period of prayer and remembrance. However, most Reform congregations hold the service only twice a year, on Yom Kippur and on the last day of Passover.

While it has become Orthodox practice for those who have not lost their parents to leave the synagog for the *Yizkor* service, this is not the Liberal habit. Liberal Judaism says that everyone should remain; we all have friends or grandparents whom we recall. And we all should remember the countless Jewish martyrs, those who "lie in far-off graves, unknown to all but God." As the origin of the Orthodox custom of leaving the synagog is only to free seats for those who had to attend, certainly where there is room all should remain.

Some Jews do not attend a *Yizkor* service until after the first year of mourning. Rabbi Solomon Freehof quotes a number of eminent Orthodox scholars who held "it is especially meritorious to participate in *Yizkor* during the first year of bereavement" (*Reform Jewish Responsa,* p. 178). Certainly, this would be true for Liberal Jews as well.

The Kohen

A *kohen* is a descendant of the House of Aaron, who were the priests in the Tabernacle and Temple of old. They had no share in the land, but lived from the tithes and other contributions of the Israelites. As they always had to be ready to conduct the Temple sacrifices, it became the custom for them not to contaminate themselves. Ritual contamination required elaborate ritual cleansing. After the destruction of the Second Temple in the year 70, their role was diminished. In Orthodoxy, it consists of being called to the Torah-reading first, the pronouncement of the Priestly Blessing on festival days, and the redemption of the first-born at the *pidyon ha-ben* ceremony.

Despite the fact that these are their only duties or privileges, they are constrained by Orthodoxy to retain their priestly purity so as to be ready to resume their functions when the Messiah should come. Therefore *kohanim* are prohibited to marry a divorced woman or convert, and to come into contact with the dead.

This means that a *kohen* will not attend any funeral except that of his own parents, nor will he enter a cemetery or a house which contains a corpse. Orthodox synagogs have been known to refuse to engage a rabbi who is a *kohen,* for he could not conduct funerals for the members of the congregation.

Reform Jews do not honor the ancient role of the *kohen* for two reasons. The first is often mentioned by the Orthodox, and is that no one really knows whether families whose names are Cohen or Kahn or Kaplan or Katz, etc., really are *kohanim.* During the many centuries names have been changed or garbled and few records have endured. The other reason is that Reform Jews do not look forward to a restoration of sacrifices and the priestly cult. The Reform conception of the messianic era is one of peace and justice and holiness for all mankind. Though we hope that Israel and Jerusalem will stand as the center of universal worship, when many peoples shall flow unto the mountain of the Lord's house (Micah 4:1), no Reform Jew contemplates the resumption of animal sacrifice. As the *kohen* will have no special duties beyond those of any other Jew, there is no reason why he should endeavor to preserve the ancient laws concerning contamination. Therefore Reform Judaism maintains that a *kohen* may attend the funeral of anyone dear to him, participate in the service and in the interment.

The Jewish Calendar

When the Israelites came into the land of Canaan and settled there, they became farmers, and they began to divide the year by its agricultural phases: plowing, sowing, harvest, vintage, threshing, etc. The months came later.

Shlomo Zalman Ariel, ENCYCLOPEDIA MEIR N'TIV, p. 247

No discussion of Jewish holidays is possible without a discussion of the *luach,* the Jewish calendar. Basically, it is a lunar calendar. The months are determined by the new moon, which comes every twenty-nine or thirty days. So the first *seder* of Passover and the first night in the *sukah* at Sukot are always on the night of the full moon, as they come on the fifteenth of the month, which is exactly the middle of the month.

Such a calendar used regularly would, however, be almost eleven days short each year. To make up for this and to restore the calendar to its approximation of the solar calendar, a leap year occurs seven times in each cycle of nineteen years, every two or three years. The Jewish leap year adds another month (*Adar Sheni* or Second Adar). This month too begins at the new moon and lasts for twenty-nine or thirty days.

The Jewish corrected calendar is in contradistinction to the Islamic which is a non-corrected lunar calendar, and therefore is the same eleven days shorter than the solar year. As the Muslims do not correct by adding a month, their holidays fall at different times of the year. Our Yom Kippur will always

117

We count the Omer from Pesach to Shavuot

come in late September or early October. The Muslim fast of Ramadan will come at any season.

There is also another slight modification of the Jewish calendar. So that Yom Kippur will never fall on a Friday or a Sunday, as it would make preparation of food difficult, and as Hoshana Rabah cannot fall on the Sabbath, as it would make impossible the ancient custom of striking willow-twigs against the synagog benches, a day is added or subtracted at Tishri time. The rules for formulating the *luach* have been established since the fourth century. Ever since then the rules for setting the holidays have been clear, and it is simple to lay out a calendar for the years to come. Volumes of calendars for the last hundreds of years and the next hundreds of years are readily available. Liberal Jews use the traditional calendar in determining when the holidays fall. Any divergence would lead to a complete sundering of the house of Israel.

Anno Mundi

The Jewish year, which is now in the five-thousand-seven-hundreds is based on the ancient conception of *li-tzira,* the traditional date of the creation of the world. The Latin name is *anno mundi,* the year of the creation of the world. The rabbis added up the figures of the various ages of the eminent men who are mentioned as the generations of Adam, trying to determine when each fathered the next, and evolved a date which satisfied them, 3760 years before the beginning of the Common Era.

The year when written in Hebrew leaves out the 5000 mark. It is considered understood. To compute any year, add the numerical value of the Hebrew letters and add 5000. To find the equivalent according to the secular calendar, add the numerical value to the number 1240. However, the first few months of the Hebrew year will always be one year ahead, as the Hebrew year begins earlier.

Two Days or One?

A constant difference in holiday observance between traditional and Liberal Jews has to do with the number of days of observance. For instance, most Liberal Jews observe only the first and seventh days of Pesach as holidays; Orthodox Jews, the first two and the seventh and eighth. Orthodox Jews observe a two-day Shavuot; Reform, only one. The reason for this discrepancy is rooted in the way the calendar was set in ancient days. The new month had to be established at the close of the previous month. Because the lunar month may have twenty-nine or thirty days, the only way its close could be determined was by watching for the new moon. The appearance of the sliver of the new moon would mean that the new month had begun. The *Sanhedrin,* the rabbinic court, sat waiting in the Court of Hewn Stone. The wood for a gigantic fire was arranged just outside, on the summit of Mount Moriah. Observers were posted.

As soon as the watchers saw the new moon they dashed in to the assembled court, attested to the moon's appearance, and the *Sanhedrin* officially declared the *Rosh Chodesh,* the inception of the new month. A torch was hurled into the piled wood, and within minutes an answering fire would be seen at the top of every high hill in Judea. Thus everyone knew that the new month had begun.

But even in ancient days most Jews lived outside of Israel, in Babylonia or Alexandria or Rome. They could not be sure which was the correct day. As the *Rosh Chodesh* came in a thirty or thirty-one day cycle, they observed both days of any holiday that came during that month, just to be sure that they had the correct day. The rabbis decided that this would be the custom for all Jews outside the land of Israel, and this continued in force even after astronomy made it possible to predict the exact phases of the moon for years in advance.

Therefore the rule is that traditional Jews of the Diaspora celebrate every holiday with an extra day, except Yom Kippur, as it would be asking too much to double the length of the great White Fast. The Jews of Israel celebrate each holiday only one day, except for Rosh Hashanah, which they too celebrate for two days. When a traditional Jew from outside of Israel goes there for a visit, he is enjoined to celebrate any holiday that occurs during his sojourn for the number of days he did in his home country. So, visitors to Israel at Pesach time will observe two *sedarim* while all about them the native Israelis are celebrating only one *seder*. If the visitor should decide that he is to become a permanent resident of the land, he immediately becomes responsible only for the one-day holiday.

For the most part, Liberal Jews accept the fact that there is no real exile or Diaspora today wherever men are free. Most Liberal Jews are content with the biblically ordained length for all of our holidays: one-day holidays remain one day; week-long holidays do not have an extra day added. However, there are Liberal Jews who do observe Rosh Hashanah for two days, because this is done even in Israel. And there are many who observe two *sedarim* at Pesach time, if only because the joy of the holiday is so great it cannot be encompassed in one day.

Holidays and Festivals

Our Jewish festivals are exceedingly ancient, in some ways even older than Judaism itself. The three pilgrimage festivals, Sukot, Pesach, and Shavuot, can be traced to the dim past. They are nature festivals, celebrating the early harvest, lambing time, and the late harvest. They had become part of what Jung called the folk-consciousness, part of the folk soul. Even in early years they had become part of Judaism by being related to Jewish history: Pesach with the freeing of the slaves; Shavuot with the giving of the Torah; Sukot, the harvest festival par excellence, was related to the patriarchs.

The joy of the festivals is born of deep instincts in man, from the soil and the round of the seasons. We who are mostly city-pent lose touch with our roots. When we relinquish our ties with the earth and growing things, we lose contact with the surge of life, with the primal force of nature, we lose contact with Judaism and with God.

Bringing bright vegetables and fruits into our homes as ornaments rather than as food, as symbols of the passage of the year and the passage of time in our lives; eating as part of a religious rite and not just to ward off hunger or to pander to the appetite; coming together with our family in religious union, these are warming basic, fulfilling parts of Judaism that bring health and love and meaning into our lives.

The Sabbath

"More than Israel has kept the Sabbath, the Sabbath has kept Israel."
ACHAD HA-AM, AL PARASHAT DERACHIM, 3, p. 79

"The Holy One Blessed be He said to Moses, 'I have a precious gift called the Sabbath. I will give it to Israel'" (*Shocher Tov* 92).

The Sabbath has been for Israel these three millennia and more the chief of days. "A foretaste of Paradise," said our fathers (*Genesis Rabah* 17:7). It was not merely a day of rest; it was the day of spirit, of holiness, of creative leisure.

According to the sages God did indeed take seven days to create the world, not just six, for on the seventh day He created the Sabbath and its rest. The Sabbath is not a mere negative refraining from work. It is, as the *Kiddush* states, the first of God's holy convocations. Its purpose was to introduce into the life of man a sense of holiness (*Rashi Genesis* 2:1).

And though the prohibitions that became part of its observance were many, to the traditional Jew they were never a burden. Rather was the Sabbath a day of delight. It brought a sense of joy so great that to appreciate it fully, the Jew was endowed with an extra soul, a *neshamah yeterah,* said Shimon ben Lakish (*Betza* 16a).

123

Blessed are You, Lord, hallower of the Sabbath

Only the Day of Atonement is more important than the Sabbath in the Jewish calendar. The Sabbath is the only holiday mentioned in the Ten Commandments. When Rosh Hashanah falls on the Sabbath, the *shofar* is not blown in traditional synagogs, even though the Hebrew name of our new year in the Torah is *Yom Teruah,* the Day of Blowing. On the Sabbath of Sukot the *lulav* is not shaken. All fast days which fall on the Sabbath, other than Yom Kippur, are postponed to the following day or advanced to the preceding Thursday. And why Thursday rather than Friday? Friday is needed to get ready for the Sabbath.

There is no parallel to the Sabbath in other ancient religions. The Babylonians had a number of days each month which were unlucky. One did nothing on these days as it was bound to turn out wrong, but they were not days of holiness, prayer or of joy. They were numerous equivalents of Friday the thirteenth. The Jewish Sabbath is unique.

The Sabbath has ever been the day when a Jew felt most Jewish. In the ghetto or in the Arab *mellah,* the Sabbath became the cornerstone of existence, the only bright day in a week of poverty and persecution. The Midrash speaks poetically and truly when it applies the words of the Song of Songs, "I am black but comely" (1:5), to Israel's Sabbath transformation: "I am black on weekdays, but comely on the Sabbath" (*Song of Songs Rabah* 1:5;2).

There was no quality of Blue Sunday to the Jewish observance of the Sabbath, though the prohibitions were many. Holiness, worship, study, human freedom and dignity, the bliss of family life, hospitality, peace, spiritual satisfaction, the enjoyment of good food and drink, these are the edifying and satisfying values that accrued from the Sabbath.

The Greeks and Romans could not comprehend the seeming wastefulness of the Sabbath. Seneca spoke out to say, "By taking out every seventh day, they lose almost a seventh part of their life in inactivity." Rather than feel that he had lost by resting, the Jew felt that he had gained immeasurably. And not only he and his family rested, so did his servants and his beasts as well. All rejoiced in this day. Slowly, through Judaism's daughter religions, Christianity and Islam, most of the rest of the world learned the blessing that is the Sabbath.

The Bible and the Sabbath

The biblical restrictions were few: "Let no man go out of his place on the seventh day" (Exodus 16:29); and "You shall kindle no fire throughout your habitations on the Sabbath" (Exodus 35:3). Indirectly the rabbis derived other prohibited activities. When the Israelites were commanded to do their cooking and baking on the sixth day for the seventh, the rabbis deduced that these were prohibited on the Sabbath (Exodus 16:23). Similarly they reasoned that gathering wood was not allowed (Numbers 15).

The rabbis noticed that the Sabbath ordinance is given right after the instruction for the construction of the Tabernacle (Exodus 31:13–17). From this they derived that all the work that went into the Tabernacle is prohibited on the Sabbath. They evolved thirty-nine separate prohibitions in five categories, and from these extended the prohibitions. The original restrictions and those derived from them all had the force of law to the traditional Jew. The only difference between the original restrictions and those derived is that a Jew may ask a non-Jew to perform one of the derived acts, not the original restrictions (see Solomon Goldman, *A Guide to the Sabbath,* p. 22).

With the years the actual effort needed for many formerly laborious actions became negligible. But the character of the Sabbath restrictions on work continued, for it was assumed that the restriction was not on the labor involved alone, but on anything that created or changed nature. So even the tiniest bit of work was denied.

However, machines may work for the traditional Jew, if they are preset before the Sabbath begins: an electric timer to turn off or on lights or an oven; even an elevator that runs up and down all the Sabbath. (It is all right for an observant Jew to ride in an elevator as that is not travelling, but no trip in a train or motor car is countenanced, not even to the synagog.)

As these multiple restrictions leave the Orthodox Jew free for what he considers far more important, it has been a source of pride and joy to him. But these restrictions present multiple problems to the Liberal Jew. The list of the prohibited has become so great that he may feel annoyance rather than a sense of holiness.

Saturday Versus Sunday

It would be entirely wrong to say that the early Reform rabbis tried to do away with the Sabbath. The celebrated fight Rabbi Isaac Mayer Wise had in his Albany synagog arose because he demanded that his members close their stores on the Sabbath!

Years ago some American temples endeavored to shift the Sabbath from the seventh to the first day of the week. It was an attempt to get their members to observe the Sabbath, even if on another day. Living in a land where the majority rested on the first day, they thought that any day of the week would do as long as it was observed regularly and with a sense of holiness. Dissertations were written in defense of this change and talmudic quotations were torn from context. Though a number of temples still have a service on Sunday mornings, this is not because these temples hold that Sunday is the Sabbath. Their major services are on our Sabbath.

The mass of Jews recognized the danger of equating the Sabbath morning services with church services. No less a reformer than Rabbi Stephen S. Wise, who conducted a Sunday morning service for a quarter of a century at Carnegie Hall, lamented that it was a mistake. During his last years his Free Synagog held its Sabbath services on the ordained day.

Sabbath in the Home

Traditional Jews must prepare the food for the Sabbath in advance, to be kept warm in the oven. The midday meal is the *cholent*, a savory stew which simmers in its own juices for a full day. Its praises have been proclaimed by many, most poetically by Heinrich Heine.

The Jewish day begins at nightfall. So we are blessed with the eves of Sabbaths and festivals, often the most beautiful part of the holy day. The Sabbath table is set, white cloth, candlesticks, *kiddush* cup, the wine, and a decorative *chalah* cover. There are two loaves of *chalot*, a remembrance of the double portion of *manna* in the wilderness.

The Sabbath Candles

Sabbath begins before actual sundown, at least by twenty minutes, to be sure that no work is done on the Sabbath—and to prolong its enjoyment. Two or more lights are kindled at the inception of the holy day. The rabbis said there are two to mark the different phrasing of the two versions of the Ten Commandments: "Remember the Sabbath" (Exodus 20:8); and "Observe the Sabbath" (Deuteronomy 5:12). But scholars say that the second light was actually to provide greater illumination than was customary on weekdays. In some families an additional candle is lit for each child. So a home with many children will have a forest of candles ablaze.

Lighting the candles (originally oil lamps) is the prerogative of the mother. The sages said that it was her reward for the effort of preparing for the Sabbath. This is an ex post facto bit of reasoning. The Orthodox woman has to kindle the lights as her husband is in the synagog at this time, reciting the Friday evening prayers. If she does not kindle them at the proper time they will not be lit at all. This is a *mitzvah* which cannot be done after the designated time, as the kindling then would be a desecration. However, in many Reform Jewish homes the mother lights the candles at the start of the Sabbath eve meal, regardless of whether or not the sun has set. In this way the entire family shares in the candle-lighting ceremony.

The traditional mother kindles the flames and then covers her eyes as she recites the blessing. This covering makes a pretty picture, but it has its origin in a dilemma. Usually a blessing is said and then the corresponding action is done. But some rabbis held that if the woman says the blessing first, she has ushered in the Sabbath, and so is enjoined from kindling the lights! To solve this problem, it was decided that she kindle the lights, cover her eyes so that she could not see them, and then recite the blessing.

Usually she adds a prayer of her own for her loved ones at this propitious moment. Certainly this is a custom to be honored in every Liberal Jewish home, as it combines beauty, meaning and spiritual worth.

Anyone may light the candles. The rabbis said that the prerogative is the mother's (*Shabbat* 2:6). But a daughter may as well, and if no female is present, the father or a son should.

The Globe Turns

The Orthodox Jewish father returns home from the synagog after the brief Friday evening service. In Israel the hour will almost always be about 7:30 P.M., as this land is not far from the equator and thus does not have a significant change of *shekia,* time for lighting the candles, as do more northerly latitudes. In Scandinavia and Alaska, the Sabbath may come by 3:00 P.M. in the winter, and not at all in June or July. A former Air Force chaplain in Alaska informs us that by common consent it is considered never to come in earlier than 5:00 or later than 9:00.

Most Liberal Jews begin their Sabbath at dinner time on

Friday evening, especially since almost all Reform synagogs have their Friday evening services after the dinner hour. This late service is a Reform innovation, which has been taken over by the Conservative movement. There are many neo-Orthodox synagogs which hold both the usual sundown service plus a later and often larger service as well.

Father Blesses

On reaching home the traditional father blesses his children, placing his hands on each child's head in turn. He says to his sons, "May God make you as Ephraim and Menasseh" (a variant of Jacob's blessing in Genesis 48:20). To his daughters he says "May God make you as Sarah, Rebekah, Rachel and Leah," and he adds the *Birkat ha-Kohanim,* the Priestly Benediction, for sons and daughters. This too is a meaningful custom that many Reform Jews perform.

The Orthodox father then greets the Sabbath angels which traditionally accompany him home from worship (*Shabbat* 119b). This is a custom introduced by the Cabbalists. And then he speaks the verses from the thirty-first chapter of Proverbs, "A woman of valor," in praise of the Jewish wife.

The Kiddush

Then follows the *Kiddush*. The traditional father has already heard the *Kiddush* at the close of the synagog service. But the wine over which it is chanted is given to some pre-Bar Mitzvah boy. So when a Liberal Jew recites the *Kiddush* in his own home and hears it again at the temple, he is only continuing this repetition.

The *Kiddush* may be recited over grape juice. During Prohibition, Reform Jews were restricted to this innocuous drink by decision of the Central Conference of American Rabbis, while

Orthodox and Conservative Jews were able to get wine, through special dispensation of Congress. Technically *Kiddush* may even be said over beer or milk, if no wine or grape juice is available. According to ancient custom, wine is used because, like the Sabbath, it brings joy and good cheer, and is a gift of God to gladden the heart (Psalms 104:15).

The *Kiddush* has happily persisted in Liberal homes. The traditional Jew begins the *Kiddush* with the verses from the Torah which tell of the creation of the Sabbath (Genesis 2: 1–3). Otherwise the traditional *Kiddush* is the same as that in the *Union Prayer Book,* I (p. 93), except for a significant omission: *mikol ha-amim,* "for Thou hast chosen us and sanctified us *from all the nations.*" Precisely the same words occur in the first Torah benediction (*Union Prayer Book,* I, pp. 145–146) and in the festival *Kiddush* (pp. 207–209), but there they appear unchanged. Was the omission only a typographical error, as one member of the CCAR staff assured us? Or was it a deliberate omission, meant to soft-pedal particularism in Liberal Judaism? If so, why has not the Torah benediction also been changed, as it has been in the Reconstructionist prayer book (pp. 160–161), which reads: "who hast brought us nigh to Thy service"? Some congregations have restored the two words. The music to the *Kiddush* demands their inclusion.

Usually the goblet over which the *Kiddush* has been chanted or recited is passed so that everyone present takes a sip. Some families in the interest of sanitation will provide individual cups, even for the youngsters who get a few drops. The wine cup is supposed to be full, as a symbol of God's bountifulness, but this need not be extended to the young. Orthodox Jews will use *kosher* wine, wine prepared for Jews by Jews. As the reason behind this has to do with the ancient pagan practice of pouring libations for the gods, there is little need for Liberal Jews to worry about this. It is customary to use a wine from Israel, as a remembrance of the ancient Temple. And it is customary to use a sweet wine, again as a symbol of God's bounty. Whether one rises for the *Kiddush* or not seems to be a local custom. Most people do.

The Chalah

Following the *Kiddush,* the Orthodox father washes his hands at the table with the appropriate blessing. Decorated ewers and basins are often used. Most Liberal Jews content themselves with washing their hands as usual before the meal.

The regular *Motzi,* the blessing over the bread, follows. It is said over both of the *chalot.* Most Liberal Jews will have only one *chalah.*

The word *chalah* comes from the Hebrew. Originally it designated the priest's share of the dough (Numbers 15:17–21). To this day, Orthodox women will pinch off a piece of the dough when they are baking and throw it into the fire, as a reminder that the Temple does not exist and there is no priesthood to claim its share (Ezekiel 44:30). The shape of our modern *chalah* is not ancient as it is probably of medieval German ancestry. Oriental Jews use the *pitta,* Arabic flat bread, and do not know the *chalah.* To most of us, the *chalah* has become the Jewish bread and is the traditional accompaniment of Sabbath and festival fare.

The Sabbath Eve Meal

The Sabbath eve meal should always be the most sumptuous of the week. Many are the injunctions concerning this. The Talmud says, "Devote part of the Sabbath to Torah, and part to feasting!" (*Sabbath Jerusalem* 15:3).

The Talmud tells the story of Rabbi Joshua ben Hanania who was a friend of the Roman Emperor Antoninus. One day the emperor ate at the rabbi's home and marveled that the food tasted better than the repasts prepared by the royal chef.

"We have a certain seasoning called the Sabbath," said the rabbi. "Give me some," said the emperor. "It works only for him who observes the Sabbath," was the rabbi's retort (*Shabbat* 119a).

Traditional Jews end the Sabbath meal with the Song of Ascents (Psalm 126) and *benschen,* grace after the meal. And traditional Jews sing *zemirot,* Sabbath table songs. Some of these are of great beauty and have found their way into Liberal services and *Oneg Shabbat* singing.

Sabbath Worship

No Sabbath is truly observed unless we join in communal Sabbath worship. Of course one may pray alone. But from the first, it was recognized that prayer with the congregation is the proper, more meaningful way. One worshiper sustains the other. Man stands with his brother as he does in life. So the Jewish family should make attendance at the synagog a regular and important part of every Sabbath. "He who prays with the community, his prayer is acceptable" (*Berachot* 29b).

Sabbath eve services in the traditional synagog are brief, the *minchah* (afternoon) and *maariv* (evening) prayers, plus additional psalms for the Sabbath. The *amidah* (standing prayer) is reduced from nineteen benedictions to seven. All in all, it is briefer than our usual Sabbath eve service.

On the other hand, the Orthodox Sabbath morning service is much longer than our Reform liturgy. There are many additional psalms and a large section called *musaf* (additional prayers), as well as the chanting of the *sidrah,* the Torah portion of the week, and the *Haftarah,* the portion of the Prophets.

When asked why he did not try to shorten the Sabbath service, an Orthodox rabbi responded, "Would a man deliberately try to shorten his visit to his beloved? The Sabbath is a queen and we delight to visit her."

Though Liberal Jews may shorten their visit, each should delight to visit the Sabbath Queen.

Oneg Shabbat

Many synagogs, Reform, Conservative and those Orthodox which have a late Friday evening service, have a collation after the service. This may be entirely social, *zemirot* may be sung, there may be a discussion or a lecture. This new custom, the *Oneg Shabbat,* the Delight of the Sabbath, was introduced by the great Hebrew poet Chayim Nachman Bialik. However, he instituted the *Oneg Shabbat* on a Sabbath afternoon. It had been the custom for the men to gather in the synagog late Saturday afternoon for a *shiur,* study of the Talmud. Bialik saw that this left out many people who would be glad to participate in some study fitting to the day, yet meaningful to them. So he invited groups to his home in Tel Aviv for Saturday afternoon. There would be a lecture and discussion, singing, and something to eat and drink. There was always food so that the regular grace could be said before the prayers at the close of the Sabbath. This brief meal was known as the *seudah shelishit,* the third meal, and was meant to satisfy the talmudic demand for three meals on the Sabbath (Sabbath 117a). As breakfast is taken at home without a *minyan,* quorum for prayer, it does not count.

The Reform *Oneg Shabbat* is a borrowing of Bialik's innovation, switched to Friday night. Reform Judaism does not ask the fulfillment of the requirement of the third Sabbath meal, but the *Oneg Shabbat* has become a worthy addition to our Sabbath pleasure.

The Havdalah

The *Havdalah* ceremony marks the close of the day of rest. The word means "to make a distinction"—between the holy and the secular, light and darkness, between Israel and the nations, between the Sabbath and the six days of the week. For *Havdalah* we use a cup of wine or any other liquid, filled to overflowing (not just to the brim) as a symbol of blessing, a spice box and a braided candle. The *besamim,* or spice box, is often of silver and usually adorned. It frequently is in the shape of a tower or a fish or other imaginative form. Within are placed aromatic spices. Some scholars say that the spices were originally a form of incense that was lit to give comfort to the Sabbath's extra soul, the *neshamah yeterah,* which was now departing. Other scholars say the spices were considered necessary for an exigent reason. The ancients thought that the flames of *Gehenna* were banked on the Sabbath so that even the atoning souls rested. At the Sabbath's end the flames were set to leaping again, and the smell of brimstone sped over the world. The spices were to mask the fetid odor. Or perhaps those scholars are right who maintain that the spices are considered a fitting parting for the Sabbath Queen.

The plaited candle is derived from the fact that the Hebrew word for light in the benediction over the light is *meore ha-esh,* "who creates the lights of flame," and light is in the plural. Therefore the multiple candle is used. Others say that this is a moment of union of the holy and the secular, that even the mundane workaday week has its aspects of holiness, and hence the two wicks of the candle.

The *Havdalah* takes place in the home—or in the Orthodox synagog at the end of the *Oneg Shabbat* or the *seudah shelishit,* the third meal. Reform Jews may well find it a fitting end to the beauty and holiness of the Sabbath. It is always a delight in our Reform Jewish camps and at *kallah* weekends.

Melaveh Malkah

The hours of Saturday night have always had a special place in the affection of the traditional Jew, for he was reluctant to say farewell to his Sabbath Bride. The term *melaveh malkah* means "escorting the queen," and is used to signify the social meal and songfest that begins with the *Havdalah* and continues well into the night. It is more lighthearted than the Sabbath afternoon *Oneg Shabbat* of the Orthodox and is a time for stories and dancing as well as for good food and endless singing. So when Liberal congregations hold a dance on a Saturday night, if only they begin with *Havdalah* they are in a good traditional spirit.

Sabbath Observance

The details of Sabbath observance vary even among our more traditional brethren. For instance, in the *Meah Shearim* section of Jerusalem, on a Sabbath afternoon, you will see many ultra-Orthodox couples proudly pushing a baby carriage. Yet other traditional Jews who are not quite so rigorous in their interpretation of Jewish law, will not hear of walking a baby carriage on the Sabbath. In B'nai B'rak the streets are actually chained off so that there is no possibility of vehicular movement on the Sabbath.

All essential services continue in Israel, but in most cities anything deemed non-essential halts. The water and electrical services continue, the phones are automatic so they will work, but buses, trains, all stores and amusement places are tightly shut. Nursing and medical care continue in the hospitals. Ambulances move freely when needed. Even the most Orthodox approve. But otherwise all regular activity ceases. Most willingly, the traditional Jew separates himself from much that most Liberal Jews consider necessary, the telephone and radio, all mechanical transport, and even walking further than a short stroll (for then it becomes travel and not just a walk), cooking, smoking and much more. Most traditional Jews consider that little has been lost and much gained by this deliberate and willing abstention: time for reading and study, for family warmth and prolonged worship, time to allow holiness to permeate our existence.

Recognizing the importance of this motivated acceptance of Sabbath restriction as essential to the Orthodox, most Reform

Jews have no desire to emulate them. How then shall he observe the Sabbath? Are there Liberal restrictions? Is there complete license?

Liberal Observance

The Sabbath must have meaning to you and your family. The meaning must be positive, of spiritual worth. Each Liberal Jew should accept a pattern of living for the Sabbath which will set it aside, to some degree, from every other day of the week.

Regular work should not be performed on the Sabbath, if possible. Even those who find that they must work should try to set aside at least a part of the evening or the day to Sabbath. Worship, especially Reform Jewish worship, is not lengthy, and even those who work will find that they can participate in the service if the desire is there.

Otherwise, reading, studying, whatever enlarges the mind and the spirit, these are the proper uses of the Sabbath. But just as the traditional scholar does not study his usual material on the Sabbath, the writer or painter or scholar who considers himself a Liberal Jew should not use the Sabbath for his usual work. Digging in a garden may be a soul stretcher to some people, especially those who work indoors all week. But to save the garden chores for the Sabbath is scarcely in the spirit of the day.

Similarly, heavy household tasks should not be done, nor should there be elaborate cooking. The Sabbath should not be set aside as a day for shopping. Visiting relatives and friends, enjoying the warmth of the family hearth, these are fit Sabbath occupations. A museum, a concert, a stroll in pleasant surroundings, games whether active or sedentary, all are permissible. In Jerusalem itself there are soccer games every Saturday afternoon. For the rabbinic statement is clear: "The Sabbath was not given but for joy" (*Pesikta Rabati* 23).

Fundamental to the day is its holiness. It should have the

feeling of being set aside from all other days, even from any other day of leisure. It should be approached with a sense of dedication, of deliberately making a part of our life and our destiny *kadosh,* holy.

The late chief rabbi of the British Empire, Dr. J. H. Hertz, in his commentary to the *Daily Prayerbook* (p. 341), tells how the Falashas of Ethiopia were harassed by missionaries to convert. They were taunted and asked to name the Savior of the Jews. They answered: "The Savior of the Jews is the Sabbath!"

High Holy Days

The *Yomin Noraim,* the Days of Awe, are the ten days of penitence when each of us is called upon to reassess the values of life and to consider how its quality may be improved. They begin with Rosh Hashanah, the new year, and close with the Day of Atonement. To the traditional Jew this is a period of the utmost solemnity, to be approached with fear and trembling. On Rosh Hashanah he is judged; on Yom Kippur the judgment is sealed. During the entire month of Elul, which precedes the new year, there are *techinot* and *pizmonim,* special penitential prayers, of soul searching, of seeking forgiveness from man and from God. The keynote of the period is its feeling of solemn atonement, yet it is mixed with a spirit of quiet confidence in which man places his trust in God. So the overall feeling is not one of sadness. At the end of the services of Yom Kippur, as soon as the fast is broken, the Orthodox Jew immediately sets out to construct his *sukah.* The future beckons. His faith admits no other course. He has done his best to atone. God has made His decision. Man can but plunge ahead.

Seventh or First

For two thousand years and more, Rosh Hashanah has been observed by the Jewish community as the Day of Judgment and as the new year festival. Yet, according to the Torah,

139

Nisan, the month of Pesach, is alluded to as the first month. The holiday we call Rosh Hashanah is designated for the middle of the year: "In the seventh month, in the first day of the month, shall be a solemn rest unto you, a memorial proclaimed with the blast of the *shofar,* a holy convocation" (Leviticus 23:23).

How did this holiday come to be associated with Tishri, and Tishri as the first month? Scholars believe that the original holiday of the seventh month was the beginning of the harvest festivals. We know that Ezra the Scribe read the Torah to the assembled people on this day (Nehemiah 8). Ezra associated the festival with the idea of renewal, of resolve to obey the Law of God, which was to be the dominant theme of Rosh Hashanah. No one knows precisely how, but Tishri became known as the first month, and Nisan, the month of the spring, became the seventh. The Jews during the Exile in Babylonia had picked up the names of the months there, and we still use them in our Hebrew calendar. The Babylonian name Tishri appears to be derived from the root *seru,* to begin.

There are four names for this festival: Rosh Hashanah, the head or beginning of the year; *Yom Teruah,* the Day of Sounding (of the *shofar*); *Yom ha-Din,* the Day of Judgment; and *Yom ha-Zikaron,* the Day of Remembrance.

Selichot

According to rabbinic legend, Moses ascended Mount Sinai to receive the second pair of tablets of the commandments on the first day of Elul. He remained there for forty days, descending on Yom Kippur (*Pirke d'Rabbi Eliezer* 46). During these forty days the people maintained their special devotion to penitence, charity and prayer. This established the mood for the whole month of Elul and the first ten days of Tishri. In Orthodox synagogs the *shofar* is blown at the end of each morning service to awaken thoughts of penitence (Rema, *Orach Chayim* No. 581). In many European communities the *shul klopper,* a man whose duty it was to go about and knock on shutters to waken the men for morning services in the days before alarm clocks, would waken everyone an hour earlier. The congregation would then gather in the *shul* for the additional *selichot,* penitential prayers. Most of these *piyutim,* special poetic prayers, are medieval works by liturgical poets of Italy, the Rhineland, France, North Africa and Palestine.

At midnight of the Saturday before the new year there is a special *selichot* service. This service is considered almost as important as Rosh Hashanah by Orthodox Jews. A number of Liberal congregations have reintroduced this service and there are special liturgies for this hour of prayer adapted by various Reform rabbis.

Most traditional Jews visit the graves of their relatives in the week before Rosh Hashanah. This is very meaningful to some people, but does not have the force of law.

The Rosh Hashanah Meal

The meal at the inception of the festival is always special, beginning with the lighting of the candles and the Rosh Hashanah *Kiddush* (*Union Prayer Book,* II, pp. 36–37). The *Motzi,* blessing over the bread, is recited over the *chalah.* Instead of the usual braided form, the *chalah* is in the form of a wheel to symbolize the wheel of life; and sometimes in form of a ladder, to represent men climbing and descending in life.

A slice of *chalah* is then dipped in honey as a hope for a sweet year to come. Or an apple slice dipped in honey is eaten, with the prayer: "May it be Thy will, O Lord, our God, and God of our fathers, to renew unto us a good and pleasant year!"

Many people eat fish at the meal, supposedly as a symbol

that their good deeds for the year may be as many as the fish in the sea. The fish is served with the head on, to express the wish: "May we be at the head and not at the tail!"

Two Days or One?

We have already mentioned the reason why most festivals are observed for two days by the Orthodox of the Diaspora but only one in the land of Israel (see p. 90). However this is not true of Rosh Hashanah. The Talmud speaks of the two days of the new year as though they were one (*Jer. Eruvin,* III end). So in Israel all traditional Jews observe Rosh Hashanah for two days. Because of this ambiguity there are some Liberal temples which observe both days, though most observe it only for one. This is a decision which each congregation makes for itself.

Tashlich

Traditional Jews have a custom which is strange to most Liberal Jews. It is based on a verse in the Prophets, "Thou wilt cast all their sins into the depths of the sea" (Micah 7:19). On the afternoon of the first day of Rosh Hashanah (the second day, if the first falls on the Sabbath), they go to a river or lake. They empty their pockets of crumbs which they have put there for this purpose and shake the hem of their coats. They recite penitential prayers.

No one knows for certain how old this custom is, but it is not mentioned until the fifteenth century. Many prominent rabbis such as the Gaon of Vilna preferred to remain at home and spend the afternoon reading Psalms or studying.

Rosh Hashanah and Yom Kippur are the two holidays which are observed more in the synagog than in the home. But the real import of these Days of Awe must lie in our lives beyond the walls of the house of worship.

"The Holy One, blessed be He, said to Israel: My sons, open for Me an aperture as narrow as the eye of a needle, and I will open for you gates through which coaches can pass" (*Pesikta,* Buber ed., 163b).

The Fast of Gedaliah

When the Babylonians destroyed the Temple in 586 B.C.E., Nebuchadnezzar appointed a Jew named Gedaliah to be governor of the conquered land of Judah. Gedaliah seems to have been a good and just man. However, zealots assassinated him. The Babylonian monarch in wrath then ordered the Exile. In commemoration of the death of a good man and in sorrow at the beginning of the cruelty of the Exile, the Fast of Gedaliah was instituted on the day of his death, the third of Tishri, the day after the second day of Rosh Hashanah (Maimonides, *Hilhot Taanit,* V, 2). Although this day is observed as a day of fasting by Orthodox Jews, it has no place in the Liberal Jewish calendar.

The Sabbath of Return

The Sabbath that falls between Rosh Hashanah and Yom Kippur is called The Sabbath of Return, because the *Haftarah* portion begins, "Return, O Irael, unto the Lord thy God!" (Hosea 14:2). It is also called the Sabbath of Repentance, as it falls during the days of Repentance.

Yom Kippur

On the Day of Atonement in ancient days, the high priest would remove his handsome robes and jeweled breastplate, and clad in the plain linen of the common priest would enter the Holy of Holies. There in the heart of the Sanctuary he would pray in atonement. All rank, all adornment, all riches, were gone. Man had come to appear before God.

Judaism holds that on this day the judgment of each man is sealed, on this day his atonement must be made manifest to himself and to God. Yom Kippur is set apart for fasting and self-denial. This is the keystone of the Jewish year. As a chasidic *rebbe* said, "On this day we smite our hearts. Far more important, our hearts should smite us!"

Though in early times Yom Kippur had a service akin to the other services of the year, by the Middle Ages it had become the longest of the services by far, and it became customary for the fervent to spend the full period in the synagog. Through the night there were psalms chanted and special prayers, *piyutim.* Yet it was never completely a day of sadness. The rabbis remind us that it is a day of joy, when sin is pardoned and man is brought near to God.

The Name

In the Bible it is called Yom ha-Kippurim, Day of Atonements (Exodus 23:26). The rabbis shortened it to the singular. The word *kippur* is from the root "to scour" or "to cleanse thoroughly." Therefore to seek atonement man must first truly repent. The day itself does not atone. It is man's seeking to cleanse himself that evokes the atonement.

Fasting

Yom Kippur is the Great White Fast. For a full twenty-four hours—and it is closer to twenty-six hours, for the ardent worshiper begins his service early and prolongs its end—traditional Jews are cut off entirely from their usual pursuits. In the Mishnah we read, "On Yom Kippur, eating, drinking, washing, anointing, putting on sandals, and marital intercourse are all forbidden" (*Yoma* 8:1).

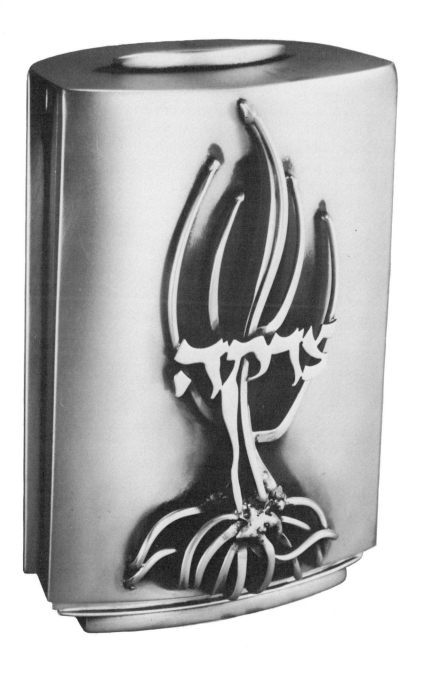

Charity saves from death

The traditional Jew wears nothing made of leather on this day. Some say the reason is that leather can only be obtained from slain animals. As the worshiper prays for mercy on this day, he should not wear anything derived from a slain beast (Agnon, *Yomim Noraim,* p. 266). Others say that as all the earth seeks repentance on this day, the earth itself becomes holy ground. And as Moses was told to remove his shoes (Exodus 3), so the Orthodox Jew removes his regular shoes (Agnon, *op. cit.,* p. 265). Liberal Jews do not usually wear different footwear.

The prohibition of washing too presents a problem to the Liberal Jew. Most Liberal Jews do wash, including the brushing of their teeth, which would not be countenanced by Orthodox Jews, as one must rinse his mouth. Most Liberal Jews would agree that as the day is not spent solitarily, as one must be with other people, one must not appear unwashed.

The reasons for fasting are four:

1. As a penance to show contrition for the wrongs we have done and for the good we have failed to do. It is a symbol of sacrifice to show that our remorse is more than words lightly uttered. Judaism does not call for an excess of self-affliction as an approach to God, but a one-day fast is considered an act affirming man's sincerity.

2. As self-discipline, to show that our vows of repentance are valid, that we can rein in our passions.

3. As a means of focusing on the spiritual. We are not supposed to think of worldly thoughts, neither of business nor pleasure, not even of food or drink. So there is the saying that Jews can be compared to angels on Yom Kippur, for then, clothed in white, they spend the day in worship.

4. As a means of awakening compassion. By suffering the pangs of hunger ourselves, we become more perceptive of the needs of others and are moved to wish to help them.

As part of fasting, food should not be handled. However, food must be prepared for children and for the sick and the aged. Children under the age of thirteen are not required to fast. The sick, even though not in danger of life, should not attempt to fast lest it delay recovery. As Rabbi Hayyim Solo-veitchik said, "It is not that I am lenient with Yom Kippur, but that I am strict with regard to saving life" (Jacobs, *Guide to Yom Kippur,* p. 25).

Liberal Jews differ among themselves on fasting. Many Reform rabbis feel strongly that all adults who are well should fast. Others say that if a person can draw near to the religious meaning of the day without subjecting himself to fasting he need not. Therefore, no hard and fast rule can be drawn for Reform Jews. However, fasting should not lightly be dispensed with for it has been an integral, meaningful aspect of Yom Kippur for millennia.

White

Orthodox Jews wear white on this holy day because they have been compared to angels. The *kittel* or *sargenes,* a long white robe, is worn as white is the color of purity, "Though your sins be as scarlet, they shall be white as snow" (Isaiah 1:18). The *Kabalah,* the mystical work, considers white the color of peace, mercy and compassion. This is why the mantles of the Torah are changed to white for the holy days.

Kaparah

An old custom was the *kaparah* ceremony on the afternoon before Yom Kippur. Each person in the family waved a cock around his head as he recited the formula, that the life of the chicken be taken instead of his own. The rooster was then slaughtered for the Yom Kippur eve meal, or it was given to charity.

Though many leading rabbis called this a superstition unworthy of Judaism, it still persists among the Orthodox. Some neo-Orthodox rabbis have suggested that the ritual be performed with money and the bill be given to charity.

Another old custom was *makot,* or *malkos* in Yiddish, lashes of a whip. In the *shtetl,* on the day before Yom Kippur, straw was laid in the synagog vestibule, and the men came to be beaten with a whip by the *shamash,* the sexton, or some other pious man. Each penitent paid a few coins for the three light lashes. The custom arose for the Torah calls for the whipping of sinners. As the lash descended the penitent recited the words of Psalm 78:38, of God's forgiving compassion. Needless to say, the beatings were symbolic, rather than a punishment.

Charity

Charity has always been the custom at Yom Kippur. In traditional synagogs on the afternoon before Yom Kippur, special plates for many worthy causes are set out on tables in the lobby and poor people gather. It is the custom to pay one's congregational dues before the service so that the worshiper may enter on his atonement devotions without any feeling of owing man or God. Then contributions were placed in the waiting plates and in the hands of the waiting mendicants. The Talmud says that the poor are considered as though they were dead (*Nedarim* 74b). Therefore the person who aids the poor and helps them to live is said to resurrect them. "He who saves one life, it is as though he has saved the world entire" (*Mishnah Sanhedrin* 4:5). This is the meaning, said the rabbis, of the expression, "Charity saves from death" (Proverbs 10:2; *Baba Batra* 10a).

The Meal

The meal on the eve of Yom Kippur is a festive meal. A piece of *chalah* is dipped in honey with the pious wish, "May God grant that this be a good and sweet year!" On this day the holiday candles are lit after the meal. If we light them before, we would usher in the fast day and thus technically be unable to eat. Memorial candles are lit just before the holiday candles. There is no *Kiddush* for Yom Kippur.

The night after the close of Yom Kippur is treated as a minor festival. We are supposed to eat well. A drink is in order. Traditional Jews break their fast and then go out and begin the construction of the *sukah*. They return after a few symbolic strokes of the hammer to finish their meal. It is customary to visit friends and enjoy the night. As the Midrash says: "Go your way, eat your bread with joy. And drink your wine with a merry heart. For God has accepted your works" (*Ecclesiastes Rabah* 9:7).

Sukot

Rabbi Bunam, a chasidic sage, pointed out that Yom Kippur and Sukot are the only holidays which the Jew celebrates with all of himself. On Yom Kippur he is totally involved in prayer and atonement; on Sukot he dwells in the *sukah*. Yom Kippur stresses the spiritual side of man; Sukot the physical. So Judaism embraces both physical and spiritual, the natural union between soul and body, the twain intended by the Torah for the service of God.

Sukot comes only five days after Yom Kippur, on the fifteenth day of Tishri. It is observed for eight days by Liberal Jews the world over. Traditional Jews observe it for nine days. Only the first and the eighth days are celebrated by Reform Jews; the first and the last three by the Orthodox in Israel; the first two and the last three by the Orthodox of the Diaspora. The seventh day is Hoshana Rabah, the eighth day is Shemini Atzeret, and the ninth is Simchat Torah. Reform Jews combine Shemini Atzeret and Simchat Torah and celebrate both on the eighth day.

Sukot is officially referred to as *zeman simchatenu,* the season of our rejoicing, and is the archetype of all thanksgiving festivals. Sukot comes after the major grain harvest. Man pauses from his work and surveys the work of his hands, the harvest he has stored, and gives thanks. "And you shall rejoice in your feast, you, your son and your daughter, and your man-servant and your maid-servant, and the Levite and the stranger, and the fatherless and the widow, that are within your gates" (Deuteronomy 16:14).

151

For the millennia since this commandment, and perhaps even before, Jews have constructed their *sukot,* booths, and have gathered the four *minim,* the four varieties of the "fruits of goodly trees," which are the symbols of the harvest, and celebrated their thanksgiving.

The Sukah

Scholars disagree as to the precise origin of the *sukah.* Tradition says that it was modeled after the temporary dwellings constructed by the Hebrews in the Wilderness, on their journey out of Egypt. Scholars say that it is actually a replica of the sun-shield erected in the fields by the ancient Hebrews after they had entered Canaan. People lived in walled towns as protection against marauders. Their fields were beyond the walls. There was a long walk each morning to the fields. In the heat of day the farmer and his helpers would eat and rest under the simple *sukah* with its roof of foliage. During the harvest season the family would live in the *sukah,* saving the long walk morning and evening, so that all could work all day. After the majority of the people became town-dwellers, Sukot was thus a reminder of their agricultural beginnings.

One can still see such shelters in Israel in the fields belonging to Arabs and in other countries of the Middle East. Only when farmers can return to their homes on mechanized vehicles do such shelters become anachronisms.

The *sukah* we build today is modeled on its ancient counterpart. It must have a roof that provides shade (the root of the word *sukah*). But the *sechach,* the covering foliage, must not be laid on too thickly, as one should be able to glimpse the stars. The frame of the *sukah* may be used time and again, but the covering must be new every year. The whole family participates in the covering and decoration of the *sukah.* Its walls are bedecked with hangings and pictures, and fruit and shining vegetables are suspended from the rafters.

The ceremony most connected with the *sukah* is the *ushpizin,* a formal invitation to hospitality. The master of the house welcomes our forefathers to join him—in spirit; and invites his friends and neighbors to join him in the meals served in the *sukah.* In the words of Rabbi Moses Cordovero, "A man should rejoice in the *sukah,* and greet his guests with joy . . . for the *sukah* is the symbol of joy" (Fabricant, *Guide to Succoth,* p. 12).

Each Orthodox Jew tries to have his own *sukah* in his garden, on his rooftop or balcony, or even on a fire escape. There is usually a large *sukah* built at every synagog, so that the man who cannot have his own can use the communal *sukah.*

Each Liberal synagog has its own *sukah,* though some congregations construct them within the sanctuary itself. Some Liberal Jews have their own *sukah* at home, and surely it is a beautiful and meaningful custom. All Liberal Jews can take pleasure in decorating their homes with fruit and autumn foliage as symbols of the happy harvest festival.

The Four Plants

The *sukah* is not the only symbol of the harvest. The four *minim,* varieties of fruit and branch, are used within the synagog and within the *sukah:* the *lulav,* a palm branch; the *etrog,* a citron (this is a citrus fruit akin to a large lemon, and not to be confused with the fruit cake ingredient, which is a type of melon); *hadas,* myrtle; and *aravah,* willow.

These four plants are held together. The myrtle and willow fit in the reed holder for the *lulav.* They then are waved in each direction according to a set formula as given in the Mishnah. Each plant, each waving has its symbolic meaning. A handsome *etrog* has always been important. In days before rapid transportation getting an unspotted *etrog* was not simple. They were grown on the island of Corfu, as the longer journey from Palestine and the meddling of the Turks there made

Corfu a more practical source. From the Greek island they were sent all over Europe. Today they are grown in Israel and shipped by air all over the world.

Orthodox Jews try to order a set for each family and even for each male in the family. Reform Jews too find their beauty and scent add meaning and color to the holiday.

Hoshana Rabah

The word *hosannah* has come to mean in English a cry of adoration or praise or jubilation. The original Hebrew has a different meaning, "O Lord, please save!" The seventh day of the festival of Sukot is called Hoshana Rabah, the Great Prayer for Salvation. Each day of Sukot special prayers are chanted as the worshipers march in a circuit of the synagog following the Scrolls of the Torah, each man bearing the four plants. On the seventh day there are seven such circuits of the synagog. To some Orthodox Jews this day is Yom Kippur in miniature. They dress in white, fast, and spend the night of Hoshana Rabah in prayer and psalm reading. The source for this extra Yom Kippur is in the mystical *Zohar*.

Towards the close of the morning service the worshipers beat willow branches on the backs of the benches until the leaves fall. According to Rabbi Eleazar of Worms (1160–1238), this symbolized man's life. As the leaves fall from the willow, so do our years fall, and we must get us a heart of wisdom to learn to use our days well. Hoshanah Rabah is not observed with any special ceremony by most Reform Jews.

Shemini Atzeret

The words Shemini Atzeret mean "the eighth day of the closing" of the festival. Traditionally, this was the time for the *geshem* prayer, for rain. Orthodox Jews though in far-off lands

Fruit of a goodly tree

still pray for the coming of the autumnal rains in Israel. We are reminded of the words of Disraeli, "A race that persist in celebrating their vintage although they have no fruits to gather, will regain their vineyards" (Tancred).

This is the last day of eating in the *sukah* for traditional Jews. Reform Jews combine Shemini Atzeret with Simchat Torah on this eighth day.

Simchat Torah

The joy of Sukot's harvest theme closes with the gladness of Simchat Torah, the Rejoicing of the Torah, the last day of the festival. This holiday marks the celebration of the completion of the Torah cycle.

It is the custom in all synagogs to read a portion of the Torah each Sabbath in an annual cycle. The time for completion of the cycle was set on the day after Shemini Atzeret, and was called the "Day of the Book." The festivities of the day were such that by the eleventh century C.E. the name Simchat Torah was common. In the fourteenth century the custom began of completing Deuteronomy and then immediately following it by the beginning of Genesis, so that at no time could it be said that the people of Israel were not reading the Torah in their synagogs.

Gradually the other customs of the holiday were added: the seven circuits of the synagog, with many men being given the honor of bearing a Torah for a circuit, the procession of children carrying colorful flags, often adorned with an apple and a lit candle on top; the calling of all the children to recite the Torah blessing on the *bimah;* and even allowing women on the main floor of the synagog for this one happy day.

The celebration of Simchat Torah was treated almost as a marriage. The bride was the Torah. The man given the honor of reading the last verses of Deuteronomy is called the *chatan Torah,* the bridegroom of the Torah; the man who reads the first verses of Genesis is called *chatan Bereshit,* the bridegroom of Genesis.

In Liberal congregations Simchat Torah is celebrated with equivalent joy. Most congregations have a circuit or more with the Torahs, the younger children following, and they may well bear flags. The lit candles are not usual. A Reform innovation is the Consecration ceremony. All new pupils of the religious school are called to the *bimah.* There they are blessed and receive a suitable memento of the occasion. It is a fitting beginning to their studies.

The Books of the Festivals

At an early time the rabbis apportioned the *megillot,* the five small books in the third section of Scripture, the Holy Writings, among the holidays. These five books are known as *megillot,* scrolls, as they often appear separately in decorated scrolls. Each holiday has a relationship to a *megillah:* Purim to the Book of Esther; Pesach to the Song of Songs, as it speaks of the love of God for Israel and Israel for God, or so said the rabbis; Shavuot to Ruth, the pastoral work; Tishah B'Av to Lamentations, which tells of the destruction of the Temple; and Sukot has Ecclesiastes. The relationship of this philosophic work is not as clear as are the other books to their festivals. Most scholars feel that the philosophy of Ecclesiastes, even its cynicism and reminders of the vagaries of life, are specifics for man in the abundance of the harvest.

These candles which we light

Chanukah

Until recently Chanukah was a minor happy holiday. It was a time for nuts and dreidels, Chanukah *gelt* and games. Even Purim was more important. The victory of Judah the Maccabee over the Seleucid Greeks in 165 B.C.E., the cleansing and dedication (*chanukah*) of the Temple, were historic facts. Ever since that triumphant celebration Jews have lit their *menorot* in happy remembrance, and every Jewish boy has dreamed of being another Judah. Yet only during the actual lighting of the candles is there a true feeling of holiness. And only during the time that the candles are lit are even the most Orthodox constrained from work. The holiday is minor, but the happiness of the people has always been real and pervaded the eight days of festivity.

Gift-giving was never truly a Chanukah feature—Purim was the period of *shalach manot,* the exchange of gifts. But we American Jews, in our desire to counteract the lure of Christmas, have added extensive gift-giving, decorations of the house, and the sense of an important holiday.

The original story of the Festival of Dedication is found in the apocryphal books of Maccabees I and II. There are actually two more books named Maccabees, but they wander far afield. This is our only holiday, therefore, which has no biblical basis. The major reason is that the Scriptures were completed but not canonized, when the celebration of this festival began. An additional consideration is the fact that the later Hasmoneans, the dynasty of the kings of Judea who were of the family of Judah and his brothers, proved to be unworthy monarchs and implacable enemies of the Pharisees and their leaders, the rabbis. The Hasmoneans' still fresh outrages against the rabbis made the memory of their ancestors suspect. So the holiday found a fixed place in the affections of the Jewish people, but the works detailing its history remained outside the canon.

Incidentally, the story of the so-called miracle, the vial of oil that burned for eight days, is not found in the books of Maccabees. It is in the Talmud (*Shabbat* 21b).

In the *Shulchan Aruch* of Joseph Karo, we find these admonitions concerning the observances of Chanukah:

"Eat and be merry. Linger over your meals and join in jest and song and tales of miracles.

"Buy yourself a *menorah* of silver to reflect the shining light. Each light should burn at least half an hour. Set the *menorah* where all can see it.

"Place the eight lights in a straight row, since no day of Chanukah is superior to another. Only the *shamash*, the kindler and guardian of the lights, stands above his brothers.

"Kindle the lights before any member of the household goes to sleep.

"Light the *shamash* and then recite the blessings. Kindle the first light on the left; move to the right. (The candles are placed from the right, but lit from the left.)

"Men and women and children may kindle the *menorah*. In some households, each person has his own *menorah* to kindle.

"Add to your usual contributions to charity at Chanukah time, so that all your brethren may share in the happiness."

The *Shehecheyanu* blessing is pronounced only on the first night of Chanukah. The first two blessings are recited each of the eight nights.

The hymn *Maoz Tzur,* Rock of Ages, is of medieval origin. The prayer *Hanerot Halalu,* "these candles which we kindle," is even more ancient, and tells us that the candles are holy and not to be used for illumination. This explains the source of

Seedtime and harvest, summer and winter shall never cease

the *shamash* candle. If we do use the light of the Chanukah candles, we can say that it was the non-sacred extra candle which we used.

The *menorah* should be placed in a conspicuous spot. The Talmud (*Shabbat* 21b) tells us that it should be placed before the house or at a window so that its lights should clearly be visible.

In Israel the Chanukah *menorah* is called a *chanukiah,* to differentiate it from any other *menorah.*

The *menorah* is lit before the Sabbath candles on Friday night; and after the close of the Sabbath on Saturday night.

The Dreidel

Chanukah has always been a time for games, especially the spinning top, put-and-take game called *dreidel* in Yiddish and *sevivon* in Hebrew. The four Hebrew letters of the top are the initials of *Nes Gadol Hayah Sham,* "a great miracle happened there." In Israel, the fourth word is *Po,* "happened here."

Latkes

The custom of eating *latkes,* potato pancakes (*levivot* in Hebrew), is derived from an even older custom, the eating of cheese pancakes. The cheese pancakes have their basis in the apocryphal story of Judith. This story is considered pertinent to Chanukah because in it the enemies of the Jews were foiled because of the bravery of an observant Jewish woman. Judith supposedly fed the pancakes to Holofernes, the general of the invading Assyrian army, to make him thirsty. When he was drunk, she dispatched him and thus saved her people. Rescuing Jews from invading idolators links the Judith story with Chanukah, and hence the custom of eating pancakes on Chanukah.

Tu Bi-Shevat

Tu Bi-Shevat or Chamishah Asar Bi-Shevat, the fifteenth day of the month of Shevat, marks the first day of spring in Israel, just six weeks after Chanukah. The *Mishnah* refers to this minor holiday as *Rosh Hashanah le-Ilanot,* the New Year of the Trees. As such, it is the Jewish Arbor Day. It is observed with gladness in Israel by planting trees. In Israel, where aridity is a constant danger, planting trees was made a holy act.

Jews in the Diaspora participate in Tu Bi-Shevat by contributing to the Jewish National Fund so that trees may be planted in their name.

In the days of Ahasuerus

Purim

Twenty-three hundred years ago there lived a virulent anti-Semite in the imperial city of Shushan of the Medes and Persians. Haman's influence on the weak monarch Ahasuerus led to a decree to slay all the Jews in the empire. The date of the massacre was set by lot, *pur* (hence the name of the holiday), for the thirteenth day of the month of Adar. But the fortunate intervention of Queen Esther, a Jewish girl, the cousin of the good Jew Mordecai, averted the evil decree. Celebrating their rescue became a holiday, and a book named after the heroine of the story was written and found a place in our Scriptures. It is the only book of the Bible without the name of God mentioned even once.

A century later this lapse was rectified in a work that purported to be the original prayers of Esther and Mordecai. It can be found in the Apocrypha.

The date set by Haman for the massacre, the thirteenth of Adar, is considered a fast day by Orthodox Jews, *Tzom Esther*. To avoid fasting, many of the Orthodox arrange the finishing of the study of a tractate of the Talmud on that day. This is called a *siyum,* and the joy of a *siyum* is such that it takes precedence over a minor fast, and a festive meal is shared by all present at the study-session.

The next day is the holiday of Purim which commemorates the deliverance. The day after Purim is also a minor holiday for the Orthodox, Shushan Purim, as it is the day on which the Jews of Shushan celebrated their deliverance.

165

The eve and day of Purim are most happy, perhaps the gayest of the Jewish year. The *Megillat Esther,* the Scroll of Esther, is read in the synagog. *Greggers,* decorated noisemakers, are rattled or spun whenever the name of wicked Haman is pronounced. After the services, mummers go about in costume to present serious and less than serious dramatizations of the story. In traditional circles, the Purim *badchan,* or jester, tells stories and makes jokes which are irreverent and completely in the spirit of this boisterous night and day.

The Purim carnival in Tel Aviv has become a three-day festivity, replete with parades, masking, costumes and much merriment. People journey from all over the country to witness the elaborate floats. The carnival is called *adloyada,* and derives its name from the Talmud (*Megillah* 7b), which commands us to enjoy ourselves as we celebrate Purim.

A decorated *megillah* was often a treasure of the Jewish home. Each *megillah* must be hand-written, and it is often hand-decorated as well.

Another traditional feature of the holiday is *shalach manot,* the giving of gifts. Usually these are baked goods, rather than anything costly, but children receive gifts.

Most Reform temples have carnivals for the children, costumes are worn, and plays and masques are presented. Often there is a party or a dance for adults as well. Yet, Purim, with all its jollity, never was nor is a major holiday of the Jewish year.

Mordecai the Jew who sits at the King's gate

The watchnight of the Lord to all Israel

Passover

Pesach or Passover has always been one of the happiest and busiest seasons of the Jewish year. In many ways it was the high point of the year. Not only did it celebrate the historic and religious meanings of liberation and freedom and the establishment of the Jewish people, it brought the promise of spring. Everyone received some item of new clothing as part of the festivities. And every aspect of the holiday, even the arduous preparation, became a joy.

Pesach was one of the few times of the year that the rabbi would preach, on *Shabbat ha-Gadol,* the Great Sabbath, just preceding Passover. His topic was always the special *kashrut* necessitated by the stringent laws prohibiting *chametz,* leaven. To achieve this special *kashrut,* the housewives were indefatigable, for the whole house had to be made *pesadig,* free of leaven, and ready for the festival.

Some traditional homes even today contain a separate kitchen, complete with stove, pots, pans, silverware (two sets of everything as usual, for *milchig* and *fleishig,* dairy and meat meals). This special kitchen is used just eight days a year, for Passover. Most homes, which have only one kitchen, have to be thoroughly scrubbed. All the usual dishes must be put away, and the Pesach sets taken out, cleaned and made ready. Poor families who cannot afford two extra sets of kitchenware and cutlery have to *kasher* their usual utensils by plunging them into boiling water. But almost all Orthodox families try to have at least a *pesidige fleishig* set, their very best usually, for the two *sedarim.*

The night before the *seder* the traditional mother carefully places ten bits of bread in obvious places. Then the father begins his *bedikat chametz,* his search for the leaven. He brushes the pieces of bread into a wooden spoon with a feather. The next morning he burns them, a sign that the home is completely free of leaven.

As the rabbis said that it is forbidden even to own leaven at Pesach, another traditional task is to "sell" all leaven, which means the regular dishes and pots and pans, for they are used for leaven all the year. If the man is a merchant, any leaven in his stock must also be "sold." This symbolic sale is effected through the rabbi. He sells all the leaven in the possession of members of his congregation to a non-Jewish person. The new owner, of course, takes only symbolic ownership, and "sells" back everything to the rabbi at the close of the festival.

The same problem arises for Orthodox Jews in the land of Israel at the approach of the *shemita,* the sabbatical year. According to the scriptural ordinance, the land is to lie fallow every seventh year. As the economy of the country prohibits this, the Orthodox rabbinate sells the entire country to an Arab, symbolically of course. The Jews then "rent" the land back from him, and the Jewish Orthodox farmer may work it, as it is not supposedly his. It is the Orthodox way to avoid consequences of a biblical ordinance which made sense in ancient days but which would be calamitous today, yet not dispensing with the law altogether.

The question of Liberal Jewish observance of the *kashrut* aspect of Pesach is not easy to answer. Those who keep the traditional *pesidige* restrictions find satisfaction in all their ramifications. However, there are many whose observance is limited to the symbolic rather than the literal approach.

For the less observant, the house should be cleaned of all breadstuff, and any cookies or macaroni products placed in a closed cabinet until the end of the holiday. Orthodox Jews will not permit any leavened food for anyone except the seriously ill during the Pesach week. Liberal Jews allow it for the very old and very young as well. Most Orthodox Jews will not use rice or peas or beans during the holiday, while most Liberal Jews will do so.

Orthodox Jews will insist on a *hechsher,* a printed guarantee signed by an Orthodox rabbi, that a food is *kosher* for Pesach. Most Liberal Jews do not require a printed permission slip. Orthodox Jews will not eat or drink any food that might have fermented, as this is related to leavening, so they will not drink beer or champagne.

The Haggadah

The traditional *Haggadah* (from the Hebrew *haged,* tell a story) is actually a form of *midrash,* a rabbinic fanciful embellishment of the biblical story, and is almost two thousand years old. While the Temple still stood, the Pesach watch-night was observed in the ancient manner. Just as the Hebrews in Egypt waited that last night for the redemption, so in Jerusalem with robes girt up our ancestors ate the roasted lamb and recounted the story of the liberation. The Samaritans, distant cousins of the Jews, still observe Pesach in this fashion on Mount Gerizim, near Nablus, according to their own calendar.

Once the Temple was destroyed and the Romans made public observance impossible, the *seder* became a private, family affair. It was then that the *Haggadah* began to take the form that traditional Jews still use. Our modern congregational *seder* is in a way a reversion to the ancient practice of a large public *seder.* The home *seder,* then, is about nineteen hundred years old, the public, more than three thousand.

The *Haggadah* which most Liberal Jews use will be different from the traditional one, which places much emphasis on the miraculous and little on relating the holiday to the present. The *Union Haggadah* is used by many Liberal Jews; others may prefer the Reconstructionist version, or some of the many newer redactions. Extra readings have been added to even the traditional *Haggadah,* for the six million martyred by the Nazis, for the Jews of the Soviet Union who do not have our freedom, for the State of Israel. They are all in keeping with the meaning of the Festival of Freedom.

Charity

A major emphasis of Pesach is charity, the privilege and duty of the free man. Before the holiday we are enjoined to give *maot chitim,* money to provide *matzot* for the poor. Inviting poor guests to our *seder* is considered a *mitzvah,* a good deed. And in every *Haggadah* there is a brief proclamation shortly after the *Kiddush,* the blessing over the wine, that begins the festival service, the *ha lachma,* "this is the bread of affliction. . . ." These words are an open invitation to all the poor to join us at our meal. They were always spoken clearly and loudly so that they could be heard in the street. They are not in Hebrew, they are in Aramaic. The reason for not being in Hebrew is simple. When the *Haggadah* was compiled about two millennia ago, Hebrew was no longer the tongue of the common man. It was reserved for study and prayer. Aramaic was the language of the street and market place. So the rabbis declared that an invitation couched in Hebrew might well not be intelligible to the poor man, who was usually unschooled. Such an invitation would be an insult to the poor and to the meaning of Pesach. Therefore it is in Aramaic. We today should not only read these words in Aramaic and in the common language of our own streets and market places, we should ensure that the words have meaning by giving charity beforehand, that the poor may be helped.

The Seder

Every Jewish holiday has its home elements, but Pesach is celebrated mainly in the home. The services in the synagog, even among the Orthodox, are rushed so that all can return home to begin the *seder*. The word *seder* means "order," and refers to the order of the Pesach home service and meal. At his *seder,* each man is a king. To emphasize that he is a free man, robed in white he reclines on cushions which soften his chair.

The table is spread with a white cloth, candles, the best silverware and china—and with the symbols of the feast. A beautiful *seder* plate with spaces for the symbols is a customary adornment, though any large plate will do.

The Fifth Cup

The four cups of wine which are drunk are to celebrate the four expressions of redemption in the Book of Exodus. Some rabbis maintained that there were five. To placate these men an extra cup of wine was placed on the table, but it was not distributed to the participants. And since it is Elijah who will answer all unsolved religious questions, this cup has been named for him. That he partakes of this cup is a legend.

The *Shulchan Aruch* says that the wine should be red, though white may be used if it is superior to the available red. In many parts of Europe white wine was used exclusively as the red wine permitted the dread canard of Jewish use of Christian blood. As recently as 1912 in the Mendel Beiliss trial in Kiev, a Jew was formally charged with the murder of a Christian boy to use his blood for Passover. The Nazis did not fail to publicize this libel. And even today scarcely a year passes that does not see its publication somewhere in Russia. Today we may use red or white wine, as we choose. Traditionally it is a sweet wine, to emphasize the sweetness of freedom.

The Plagues

Some Reform versions of the *Haggadah* omit the enumeration of the ten plagues, as we do not like to rejoice in the suffering of our enemies. One is reminded of the *Midrash,* that when the angels rushed to sing paeans of joy when the Egyptians were overcome, God stopped them, saying, "What, my creatures are drowning, and you would sing!" (*Megillah* 10b).

There is a custom that when the plagues are enumerated a finger is dipped into the cup and a bit of wine is dropped into the saucer. The usual reason given for this old custom is that we thus show our sympathy with those who suffered by diminishing the wine we drink. Whether a Liberal Jew will enumerate the plagues at his own *seder* and dip his finger is a matter he should decide in advance.

Afikoman

The middle of the three *matzot* is broken and half of it distributed early in the *seder*. The second half is hidden, tucked away among his cushions, by the father. The service after the meal begins with the eating of some or all of this second half of *matzah.* It has become a pleasant game for the children to attempt to filch this *matzah* and hold it until it is needed. Then the father must redeem it with a gift. Some hold that this custom is only a device to keep the children busy. Others say that it arose because the father would put this special piece of *matzah* aside lest it become mixed with the rest of the *matzah.*

This piece of *matzah* is called the *afikoman,* obviously not a Hebrew word. Most scholars agree that it is of Greek origin, but are not agreed as to its source. Some relate it to the word for dessert, others to the ban on entertainment after this meal, and others to a ban on visiting other families after the *seder*.

In some communities only a bit of the second half of the *afikoman* was eaten. The rest was nailed to a wall, and it was supposed to serve as a talisman of good fortune for the household.

Eggs

In addition to the roast egg on the *seder* plate, there is a custom of serving a hard-boiled egg in salt water as the first course of the meal. Some scholars regard it as a relic of the *antipasto* of Roman days. Others relate it to the hope of redemption, as the egg is considered a symbol of resurrection. The salt water is to complete the metaphor: despite our tears, yet do we find redemption!

Usually the roasted egg is used for ceremonial purposes only, but in some Oriental communities the first-born son eats it at the end of the *seder,* as a remembrance of the protection of the first-born of Israel. In other communities, the eldest unmarried daughter eats the roasted egg as conducive to a fruitful marriage.

Next Year in Jerusalem

The formal *Haggadah* closes with "Next year in Jerusalem!" The *Union Haggadah* changed this to "next year may we all be free men." Certainly this is a magnificent hope. The original line was expunged from the *Haggadah* in the early and long-outgrown anti-Zionism of half a century ago. However, some Liberal Jews may want to restore the original (or express both lines with ardent conviction), for Jerusalem has been the center of Jewish worship and aspiration for three millennia.

Even in Jerusalem itself this line is proclaimed. Some may

add the word *habenuya,* "in the rebuilt Jerusalem." Most Jews believe the word Jerusalem refers even more to the spiritual Jerusalem than to the earthly.

Lag Ba-Omer

There is a biblical ordinance concerning the counting of the barley sheaves, the *omer,* beginning at Pesach and culminating at Shavuot (Leviticus 23). On the thirty-third day of the counting of the *omer,* which corresponds to the eighteenth day of Iyar, a semi-holiday takes place. It is perhaps the most obscure day of all Jewish holidays, yet it has been celebrated with joy for at least eighteen hundred years.

It is called Lag Ba-Omer, which means the thirty-third day of the *omer,* but why it is celebrated is not clear. Legend connects it with Roman persecution and perhaps with some victory of Bar Kochba over their legions. There are some who say that it marks the cessation of a plague that decimated Rabbi Akiba's students.

It is often called the scholars' festival, bringing to mind the devotion to study of Rabbi Akiba and his students despite Roman opposition and oppression. It reminds us of those perilous days when all Jewish learning was proscribed and Jewish lads were forced to pursue their studies furtively, going into the forests to meet their rabbis while pretending that they were hunting.

No one really knows how it became a day of joy. The Orthodox use it to punctuate the period of semi-mourning which follows Pesach. The reason for the semi-mourning, too, is not particularly clear. Usually it is related to Roman persecution.

Whatever the reason, the Orthodox do not permit marriages from Pesach to Shavuot, excepting *Rosh Chodesh,* the Day of the New Moon, and Lag Ba-Omer. Some permit marriages after this day. Others insist on calling another halt until after Shavuot itself.

The day is celebrated with picnics, hikes, archery, and bonfires. In Israel bonfires brighten the night all over the country. The *Chasidim* flock to the village of Meron to visit the tomb of Rabbi Shimon ben Yohai, a second-century luminary, who supposedly died on this day.

Reform religious schools usually observe this day or the nearest Sunday to it, with hikes, picnics or other jaunts to the outdoors.

Yom ha-Atzmaut

In 1969, by formal resolution of the Central Conference of American Rabbis in convention at Houston, and of the biennial of the Union of American Hebrew Congregations in Miami, it was decided that *Yom ha-Atzmaut,* Israel Independence Day, is to be observed by Liberal Jews and synagogs. This was reaffirmed at the CCAR's first convention in Jerusalem in 1970 at a historic meeting on Mount Scopus. Israel was established on May 14, 1948, the fifth day of Iyar. Like all other Jewish holidays, we use the Hebrew calendar in ascertaining the date for celebration.

In Israel the holiday is celebrated most joyously, in the synagog, at home and in the streets. If *Yom ha-Atzmaut* falls on a Sabbath or a Friday, it is celebrated the preceding Thursday, following halachic precedent. As the day and even more, the evening before, are tumultuous with fireworks, parades, public dancing and entertainment, one can readily understand why it is not allowed to fall on the Sabbath or to interfere with preparation for the Sabbath.

Its paths are paths of pleasantness

Shavuot

Shavuot is the holiday of the first fruits, the thanksgiving for the early harvest, a time of beauty and joy. It is known as Shavuot, the Festival of Weeks, as it comes precisely seven weeks after Pesach; *Hag ha-Katsir,* the feast of the harvest; and as *Yom ha-Bikkurim,* the day of the first fruits. Beginning with the second day of Pesach, seven weeks or forty-nine days were counted by setting aside an *omer,* a measure of barley, and the fiftieth day was celebrated. The fact that it is on the fiftieth day gives it its English name of Pentecost, which is based on the Greek word for fifty.

Shavuot is one of the three pilgrimage festivals, Pesach and Sukot are the others. In the days of the Temple, Jews from all over the land and from distant lands as well, would stream up the hills to Jerusalem. Bearing their baskets of grain and almonds and early fruit, leading choice animals for sacrifice, they would come to give their thanks to God. A million people would come, we are told, yet there was always room for them all.

In ancient days an additional name and importance were given to the holiday, *Zeman Matan Torah,* the Festival of the Giving of the Torah. This has become the principal importance of the day and the Decalog is read in all synagogs at Shavuot, in remembrance of its prime proclamation.

Orthodox Jews celebrate Shavuot with joy, yet there are fewer customs associated with this day than even minor holidays. It is traditional to eat milk foods as a symbol of the

179

Torah, according to the allegorical interpretation of the Song of Songs: "Just as milk is pure, so the words of the Torah are true" (*Song of Songs Rabah* 1:2; 3).

Reform Judaism had added a third meaning to the festival of first fruits and Torah giving. It has specified Shavuot as Confirmation time, as the most fitting day of the year for this significant affirmation of Judaism.

Reform Jews continue the old custom of bringing fresh greens and fruit into the house as a symbol of Shavuot. They might well read in the Book of Psalms as ancient custom has it, in remembrance of King David who died on this day.

Orthodox Jews stay awake late on Shavuot eve, reading Psalms and special prayers. Legend maintains that when God came to Sinai to give the Torah, the Israelites were still asleep and Moses had to waken them. So today the Orthodox stay awake this night, to show there is no need to awaken them to receive the Torah.

Entreat me not to leave you

How does the city sit solitary

Tishah B'Av

In the year 586 B.C.E., and again in the year 70 C.E., after a long and bloody siege the Temple in Jerusalem was destroyed by foreign invaders. Both of these calamities occurred on precisely the same day, the ninth day of the month of Av. Was it just coincidence or part of some divine plan? The traditional Jew considers the latter the more probable. King Ferdinand signed the decree of expulsion of all of Spain's Jews on that selfsame date.

This day in the middle of the summer is the second great fast of traditional Jewry. It is a day of the most serious mourning. Neither food nor drink is allowed for the full twenty-four hours. The congregation sits on the floor or on low benches, with sandals rather than shoes on their feet. Candles are lit and the usual synagog furniture is overturned. Besides the special sad prayers for the day, the reading is from the Book of Lamentations, Jeremiah's threnody at the destruction of the Temple and the misery of the people marching slowly on bleeding feet to their captivity in Babylonia. Not even Yom Kippur is as sad as Tishah B'Av, for the Day of Atonement carries with it the feeling of atonement achieved and of faith in the future. There is a special *trop* or cantillation for this day that accents the melancholy.

The sadness is alleviated only by the prayers that look forward to the coming of the Messiah and the rebuilding of the Temple on Mount Moriah and the reestablishment of the Temple cult. Not all Orthodox Jews may look upon the reinstitu-

183

tion of sacrifice as a desired goal, but unquestionably many do. The first chief rabbi of Palestine, Abraham Isaac Kuk, established a special *yeshivah* for the study of sacrifice, in order to be ready when the *Mashiach,* the Messiah, should come.

Liberal Judaism has de-emphasized Tishah B'Av more than any other holiday. It is not that we do not mourn for the loss of life and the wretchedness of our people after these twin tragedies. We do. But most Reform Jews feel that the Temple destroyed by the Romans had become a symbol of archaic usages. Judaism's true worship service was already being preempted by the synagog; the rabbis had superseded the priests as the religious leaders of the people. The Temple's fall wrote finis to all further animal sacrifice in Judaism, as only there on the ancient site could it be performed. Prayer, charity and study of the Torah took the place of sacrifice, as they have to this day. For these reasons there is relatively little or often no observance of this day of mourning in Liberal Judaism.

Other Fasts

There are two other fasts which originate with the siege and destruction of Jerusalem: *Shivah Asar be-Tamuz,* the 17th of the month of Tamuz, which marks the breaching of the walls of Jerusalem by the Romans; and *Asarah be-Tevet,* the 10th of Tevet, the day the Babylonians began their siege. These fasts are not as strict as those of Yom Kippur and Tishah B'Av. During the Second Commonwealth *Tzom Gedaliah* and *Asarah be-Tevet* became days of festivity, and there are some people who today would turn these three minor fast days into days of rejoicing, to fulfill the prophecy that all fasts "shall be to the house of Judah, joy and gladness" (Zechariah 8:19). As the Temple is not rebuilt, Orthodoxy still treats all three as fast days.

Firstborn sons are supposed to fast on the eve of Passover, as an expression of gratitude to the Almighty for sparing the

Hebrew firstborn at the final plague in Egypt. As on *Tzom Esther* the fasting can be averted by completing a tractate of the Talmud which demands a celebration.

There are many non-ordained fasts listed in the *Shulchan Aruch* which only the pietists observe: the days of the deaths of Moses and Aaron, the day that the Torah was translated into Greek, and even the day on which Hillel and Shammai began their differences (*Orach Chayim,* Laws of Fasting, 580:1–3).

The Talmud prescribes a day of fasting for those who have had an evil dream (*Taanit* 12a). The minor fasts are observed from daybreak to sunset only, and one may work or wash during the day.

Havdalah—the holy from the secular

Glossary

Adloyada—The Purim carnival in Tel Aviv, a time of masking and rejoicing. The Hebrew means "Until he doesn't know the difference" and is from the Talmud (*Megillah* 7b), which specifies that on Purim a man should drink until he doesn't know the difference between blessed Mordecai and cursed Haman. The Hebrew essayist Achad Ha-Am gave the carnival this fitting name.

Adonai—The Lord. Originally the word meant "My Lords," the plural of *adoni,* my lord. It came to be used as the pronunciation of the Hebrew *tetragrammaton,* the four-letter name of God, *YHVH,* which occurs often in the Scriptures and the prayer book. This word was never pronounced by the Jews except on Yom Kippur, by the high priest. Instead *Adonai* was substituted. The plural form was used as a plural of majesty. Today traditional Jews will not pronounce even *Adonai,* except at worship, and will substitute *ha-Shem,* the Name, or *adoshem,* which is a meaningless composite.

Agunah—A woman whose husband has left and is presumed dead, but whose death cannot be proved or authenticated according to Jewish law. The word *agunah* is from the Hebrew, "to be shut off" (Ruth 1:13).

Aliyah (pl. *Aliyot*)—The Hebrew means "going up, ascending," and the word is used in at least three ways: (1) The going up by the people to the Temple in Jerusalem on the pilgrimage festivals in ancient days. (2) Going to live in the land of Israel, as in modern days. (3) The being called to ascend the *bimah* to assist in the Torah-reading in the synagog during public worship. In the traditional synagog seven men are called to an *aliyah* at each Sabbath service. The first is a *kohen,* a descendant of the ancient priests; the second a *levi,* a descendant of the Levitical priestly assistants; the others Israelites, Jews of no particular descent. Originally, each person who participated read his own portion of the *sidrah,* the weekly Torah reading. After a while a *baal keriah,* "master of the reading," was appointed, and each man given an *aliyah* would only pronounce the blessings before and after the Torah reading.

Amidah—The Standing Prayer. Also called *Shemoneh Esreh,* Eighteen, as it used to contain that many benedictions. For two millennia it has contained nineteen, but it still bears the ancient name. It is the central prayer of all traditional worship.

Arba Kanfot—or *Talit Katan*—A rectangular piece of linen or wool, with fringes (*tzitzit*) at its four corners, and an opening in the center to admit the head. *Arba kanfot* means "four corners"; *talit katan* means "little *talit* or prayer shawl." It is worn by Orthodox Jews under their outer garment during the day. The *tzitzit* are supposed to be reminders of the obligation to observe the commandments.

Ashkenazim—Jews of central Europe, differentiated from the *Sephardim,* the Jews who are descended from ancestors who came from the Iberian peninsula. Ashkenazic Jews have many customs which are different from their Sephardic brothers, and there are also many regional differences within the two main groups. These include differences in the pronunciation of Hebrew, in the liturgy and in synagogal practice, amongst many others.

Atarah—The embroidered collar portion of a traditional *talit,* prayer shawl. Often it contains the blessings to be recited on donning the *talit.* The word *atarah* is also used as the name of the Reform version of the *talit.* It has a pointed yoke so that it will stay in place and does not have the exact number of fringes and knots required by *halachah.*

Aufruf—A calling up, from the German or Yiddish. To be called to the reading of the Torah, especially a bridegroom at the Sabbath before his marriage.

Baal ha-Bayit—Master of the House, the Hebrew term for Mr. Average Man.

Badekens—Covering or veiling the head of the bride. This is a brief ceremony before traditional weddings, in which the rabbi, sometimes assisted by the groom, places the veil over the bride and blesses her.

Badchan—A jester, especially at Purim, and often at a traditional wedding meal.

Bedikat Hametz—Searching for leaven. Orthodox Jews cleanse their houses most thoroughly just before Passover. On the evening before the *seder,* the fourteenth of Nisan, the mother places ten pieces of bread in obvious places. The husband then follows after her and sweeps the bread into a wooden spoon with a feather. These are wrapped in a cloth and burned the next morning.

Benschen—Grace after meals. There are many forms of the traditional *benschen,* for when one dines alone or in a company, at holiday time, after a wedding or other special occasion. The word *benschen* may be from the Latin *benedicere,* to bless.

Berachah—A blessing. Any prayer that begins: Blessed are You, O Lord our God . . . is a blessing. Traditional Jews recite blessings not only as part of regular services but also many times a day, before and after eating, drinking, washing, seeing a dwarf or a king, and many, many other times.

Berit—Covenant. There are a number of covenants in the Torah: God established a Covenant with Abraham (Genesis 17); with Moses and Israel at Sinai (Exodus 19 and 20); and just before they entered Canaan (Deuteronomy 29). *Berit* is a solemn pact between God and Israel, He shall be our God; we shall be His people, to observe His commandments.

Berit Milah—The Covenant of circumcision is first commanded to Abraham: "You shall keep My covenant, you and your descendants after you throughout their generations. . . . Every male among you shall be circumcised . . . it shall be a sign of the covenant between Me and you. He that is eight days old among you shall be circumcised" (Genesis 17:9–12). This command is repeated again and again in the Torah.

Besamim—Spice box, used at *havdalah,* the close of the Sabbath ceremony. According to Maimonides, the spices are to cheer the soul which is saddened by the departure of the Sabbath. It may be of metal or olive wood. It is often in a fantastic form, a fortress with towers, a segmented fish, a winged griffin.

Bimah—A platform or stage. The pulpit area in a synagog. Most Orthodox synagogs have a *bimah* or *almemar,* a raised reading area in the center, from which the Torah and *Haftarah* are chanted. In the Sephardic synagog the entire service is conducted in the center as well. Reform synagogs have their *bimah* as a platform before the ark.

Birkat Kohanim—The Priestly Blessing. Originally this was a regular part of the daily service in the Temple. Every morning and evening the priest would ascend a special platform (*duchan*) and pronounce the words of the Torah so that they might "put My name on the children of Israel:

The Lord bless you and guard you;
The Lord cause His face to be bright upon you,
    and be gracious unto you;
The Lord lift up His countenance upon you,
    and grant you peace."   NUMBERS 6:24–27

Chalah (pl. *Chalot*)—The braided eggbread which has become the Jewish bread for Sabbath, holidays and festive occasions.

Chalitzah—The ceremony by which the brother of a man who dies childless releases the widow from the need to marry him. The removal of a shoe in public and spitting were considered insulting, and thus the widow's removal of her brother-in-law's shoe is considered a public demeaning as he has refused to marry her and thus perpetuate the dead brother's name.

Chametz—Leaven.

Chanukiah—A Chanukah *menorah*.

Chasidim—Members of the chasidic movement. A pietist and mystic brand of Judaism founded about 1750 in Eastern Europe by the *Baal Shem Tov,* The Master of the Good Name. A kind of reform movement at its inception, it soon became and remains the ultra-Orthodox wing of Judaism.

Chatan—Bridegroom.

Chatan Bereshit—The bridegroom of Genesis, the man called to the reading of the first portion of Genesis at Simchat Torah.

Chatan Torah—The bridegroom of the Torah, the man called to the reading of the last portion of Deuteronomy at Simchat Torah.

Chatunah—A wedding.

Chazan—A cantor. Originally the synagog caretaker who announced prayer time and Sabbath time from the roof. He became a combination of poet, composer and chanter of the prayers at services.

Cheder—The one-room primary Jewish school in the *shtetl*.

Chevrah Kaddisha—Organization of Holiness. The voluntary group which took care of the funeral and burial in the *shtetl*. It still persists in modern Israel and among *Chasidim* wherever they live.

Chiddush—An innovation, particularly a new scholarly interpretation of a verse from the Torah or a point in the Talmud.

Cholent—A spicy stew of meat, beans and onion, eaten at the Sabbath midday meal by the Orthodox. As no cooking may be done, and as one must eat well to honor the Sabbath, the stew is prepared the day before, covered with a tight pastry crust, and put in an oven to cook slowly for twenty-four hours.

Chol ha-Moed—The secular portion of a festival. Passover and Sukot each is a full week long. Only the first and last days (the first two and last two for the traditional) are holidays. The intermediary days which are not festival days and yet partake of the spirit of the holiday are the *Chol ha-Moed*.

Chupah—The wedding canopy.

Daven—The Yiddish word for the verb "to pray."

Derashah—Sermon or Exordium. A discourse, usually on the Torah or Talmud, a feature of the Orthodox Bar Mitzvah feast and of the wedding feast. The boy or the groom addresses the guests to demonstrate his learning.

Derashah Geschenk—Gifts given to the Bar Mitzvah or the bridegroom, usually of money, in response to his *derashah*.

Dreidel—The Chanukah put and take top. The Hebrew letters are *nun, gimel, he,* and *shin*. Each player puts in a nut or two and they take turns spinning the *dreidel*. *Nun* stands for *nichts,* nothing. *He* stands for *halb,* the spinner takes half of the pot. *Gimel* stands for *ganz,* he takes all. *Shin* stands for *shtell,* put out; he puts out the number of nuts in the pot. In Hebrew, *sevivon*.

El Male Rachamim—God Full of Compassion, a prayer for the repose of the soul of the dead. It is chanted or read at funerals or at *Yizkor,* memorial services. The words are:

> *O God full of compassion, Thou who dwellest on
> high! Grant perfect rest beneath the sheltering wings
> of Thy presence, among the holy and pure who shine*

as the brightness of the firmament, unto the soul of
(*the Hebrew name of the departed is entered here*)
who has gone unto eternity. May his repose be in
Paradise. Therefore, may the Master of Mercies en-
fold him under the cover of His wings forever, and
may his soul be bound up in the bond of life eternal.
May the Lord be his possession, and may his repose
be peace. And let us say: Amen.

Erusin—Traditional engagement.

Etrog—The citron. The Torah commands the use of four species
of fruit and green to celebrate Sukot (Leviticus 23:40). The
etz hadar or "goodly tree" is understood to be the *etrog,* which
is Aramaic for citron, a citrus fruit tree. It has been a popular
Jewish symbol since ancient times.

Fleishig—Meat, or any food that contains meat, or any utensil used
for meat.

Gan Eden—The Garden of Eden or Paradise.

Gaon—Originally the head of a talmudical academy in Babylonia.
Later used only for the greatest talmudic luminaries.

Gehenna—A place of cleansing for the wicked after death, according to traditional Judaism. *Gei ben Hinom* was the valley of
the sons of Hinom, near Jerusalem, where idolators used to sacrifice children to the bloody idol of Moloch (Jeremiah 32:35).
The area was considered cursed and after the cessation of idol
worship, the valley was used for the disposal of garbage. Hence,
there were always fires burning and a heavy pall of smoke. The
name passed into use as a designation of the place of punishment for sins in the hereafter. But the concept of hell is not accepted in the mainstream of Jewish thought, and even the Zohar,
the medieval mystical work, says that sinners are punished in
Gehenna only up to twelve months.

Gelt—Money, especially coins given to children for Chanukah.

Gomel—The blessing that is recited after recovery from a dangerous illness or return from a dangerous trip: Blessed are You, O
Lord our God, King of the Universe, who is kind and beneficent
to the bad and to the good, and has shown me every kindness.

Gregger—A noisemaker, usually a metal case that spins on a ratchet mounted on a wooden handle, creating an infernal racket. It is twirled with glee in the synagog during the reading of the Purim *megillah,* whenever the name of Haman is read.

Hachnasat Kallah—The charitable society that provided a dowry and thus enabled an impoverished young woman to become a bride.

Haftarah—Reading of the prophetic portion. The word *haftarah* is derived from the Aramaic word for "conclusion." A reading from the second section of the Scriptures, the books of Joshua through Malachai, was selected for each Sabbath and festival throughout the year. Usually this reading is related to the Torah portion of the day which it follows.

Haggadah—The telling of the story of the Exodus is the major part of the special service of the *seder,* the home ceremony and meal that marks the inception of Pesach. *Haggadah* means "recountal." The *Haggadah* also tells of the paschal lamb and its sacrifice in ancient days, and explains why we eat *matzah* and *maror,* the bitter herb.

Halachah—Law. The root of the word *halachah* means "the going," and it refers to Jewish law by which each Jew was supposed to walk. *Halachah* covers every aspect of life, business law, religious law, agricultural law, matrimonial law, and embodies all of the Jewish legal tradition. Seventy percent of the Talmud is taken up with *halachah.* The other thirty percent is taken up by *agadah,* ethical teachings, fanciful stories, and various rabbinic comments and reports. Orthodox Jews live by the *halachah.*

Ha Lachma—"This is the bread of affliction which our forefathers ate in the land of Egypt . . . Let all who are hungry come and eat," from the Passover *Haggadah.*

Havdalah—Distinguishing. The ceremony that marks the end of the Sabbath and the inception of the secular week.

Hazkarat Neshamot—Memorial service. The words mean "Remembrance of the souls" of the dead.

Hechsher—A rabbi's signed attestation as to the *kashrut* of some item.

Hesped—A eulogy.

Kabalah—The mystical tradition. Alongside normative Judaism there has always been a strong mystical movement whose importance varies from era to era. The *Kabalah* encompasses the writings, principally the Zohar, and the philosophy of Jewish mysticism.

Kaddish—The Aramaic prayer that originally was used to close a *shiur*, a study session, and which has become the traditional Jewish affirmation of faith at the time of death and a remembrance of the departed:

> *Glorified and sanctified be His great name in the world which He has created according to His will. May He establish His kingdom during your life and during your days, and during the life of all the house of Israel, speedily and soon, and say ye, Amen.*
>
> *Let His great name be blessed forever and to all eternity. Blessed, praised and glorified, exalted, adored and honored, extolled and lauded be the name of the Holy One, blessed be He; though He be high above all the blessings and hymns, praises and words of solace which are uttered in the world; and say ye, Amen.*
>
> *May abundant peace and life descend from heaven upon us and upon all Israel; and say ye, Amen.*
>
> *May He who makes peace in His heights bring peace upon us and upon all Israel; and say ye, Amen.*

Kaddish le-Ithadta or *Kaddish Yatom*—Orphan's *Kaddish* recited at graveside at traditional burial. The first paragraph only is different:

> *Extolled and hallowed be the name of God in that world which He is to create anew, and to revive the dead and to raise them to an everlasting life. Then will the city of Jerusalem be rebuilt, the Temple be erected there, the worship of idols be erased from the land, and the Holy One Blessed be He will reign in His Kingdom in majestic glory. May this happen in your lifetime and in your days, and in the lifetime of the whole house of Israel, speedily and near in time, and let us say: Amen.*

Kadesh—A sanctification, the original name for betrothal.

Kallah—There are two distinctly different meanings: (a) A bride, (b) A study session, particularly a period of days or a week set aside. In Babylonia it was a period after the harvest reserved for talmudic study.

Kapel—A skullcap.

Kasher—To render *kosher;* especially washing and salting meat to draw out all the blood, according to Orthodox *halachah.*

Kashrut—Fitness for use. As such, *kashrut* may refer to a *kosher shofar* or *kosher talit,* one that meets traditional ritual requirements. Most often the term is used for food that is ritually clean and edible.

Keriah—Tearing of garments of the mourners at a funeral. It is a sign of mourning. Conservative Jews have substituted the tearing of a black ribbon. By pinning it to the clothes it becomes part of the garb and thus satisfies the custom.

Kest—A form of traditional dowry in which the bride's father supports the couple while the groom continues his talmudic studies.

Ketubah (pl. *Ketubot*)—Marriage agreement, a formal document.

Kiddush—Making holy. The blessings chanted over the wine cup at the inception of the Sabbath and festivals.

Kiddushin—Sanctifications, traditional designation of a wedding.

Kinyan—Purchase, the legal part of a traditional wedding.

Kipah—Skullcap.

Kise Eliyahu—The Chair of Elijah. An empty chair is set aside at every traditional *berit milah* for the prophet Elijah. He is supposed to be present to see that Jews are still faithful to the covenant.

Kittel—A long white robe worn by Orthodox Jews on Yom Kippur and Hoshana Rabah and at the *seder,* and at their weddings. White is a sign of purity.

Klezmorim—Yiddish for musicians.

Kohen—A priest. A descendant of Aaron, and thus of the priests of the Temple in Jerusalem.

Kvatter (f. *Kvatterin*)—A kind of assistant godparent at the traditional *berit milah.*

Latkes—Potato or cheese pancakes.

Levi—A priest's assistant. A descendant of the tribe of Levi, and thus of the assistants to the priests in the Temple.

Levivah (pl. *levivot*)—Hebrew for latke, potato or cheese pancake.

Li-tzira—According to creation; the designation of the Hebrew year.

Luach—The Hebrew calendar.

Lulav—A palm branch. One of the four symbols of Sukot.

Maariv—The traditional evening prayers, conducted after sundown. Originally this was an optional prayer, but it was made mandatory in the Middle Ages. It may be begun as soon as three stars are visible in the sky.

Machzor—The traditional prayer book for the High Holy Days and for the festivals.

Makot—Whipping or blows. Refers to the symbolic whipping received by Orthodox Jews on the eve of Yom Kippur. Also, the Hebrew name for the plagues of the Exodus.

Maot Chitim—Wheat money. Charity to the poor to help them buy *matzah* and other foods for Pesach.

Maoz Tzur—Rock of Ages, Chanukah hymn written in the thirteenth century by Mordecai ben Isaac. The English paraphrase is by Rabbi Gustav G. Gottheil.

Mashgiach—An informed, pious Orthodox Jew who supervises the *kashrut* of the food at a restaurant, hotel or catering establishment. He will also see to it that none of the help will do any cooking or other preparation on the Sabbath.

Mashiach—The Messiah; originally, "the anointed one."

Matzah (pl. *Matzot*)—The unleavened bread eaten at Passover.

Mazal—A constellation. Two thousand years ago everyone believed in astrology. So when one said "*mazal tov,*" he was wishing his fellow "a good constellation." The word has since come to mean luck, so *mazal tov* means "good luck" today.

Melave Malkah—Accompany the Queen. The Queen Sabbath is parted from reluctantly. Therefore traditional Jews will continue to act as though observing the Sabbath after its cessation. They sing, tell stories, eat and drink in honor of the queen.

Mellah—The Arabic word for ghetto. The Jew in Arab lands was supposedly to be treated as a *dhimmi,* a protected cousin. However, most of the time they were protected only in that they were not killed. They were forced to live in a crowded, insanitary *mellah,* subject to high taxes and grave repressions.

Menorah—Seven-branched candelabrum of the Tabernacle and the Temple, often referred to as a symbol of the seven days of creation, and of Judaism itself. The seven lamps burned from sunset to sunrise. The center lamp burned all day as well, and from it is derived the *ner tamid,* the eternal light, that burns before the ark in each synagog. According to the Talmud (*Menachot* 28b), it is forbidden to use a seven-branched candelabrum except in the Temple. The Orthodox use such a *menorah,* but they are always certain that it does not look like the great golden *menorah* of the Temple.

Mezuzah—A scroll bearing the *Shema,* "Hear O Israel," and the following passages from Deuteronomy (6:4–9; 11:13–21), within a case. It is affixed to the right doorpost as a sign of a Jewish home and to ask God's blessing thereupon. Sometimes untraditionally worn as a charm on a chain about the neck.

Midrash—Multivolumed work of interpretation and embellishment of the Torah, usually of ethical importance, often fanciful, much of it quite ancient.

Milah—Circumcision.

Milchig—Food containing milk or milk products, or any utensil used for milk products.

Minchah—The traditional daily afternoon service. Originally just after noon, it was moved back so that it now comes just before evening. *Minchah* means a gift or a meal offering, and it was the afternoon sacrifice.

Minhag—Custom. The religious customs of an area would in time take on the force of law, and at times even supersede law. "Custom overrules law" (*Sofrim* 14:18).

Minim—The four plants that symbolize the harvest at Sukot: *etrog,* citron; *lulav,* palm branch; *hadas,* myrtle; and *aravah,* willow.

Minyan—A quorum. Ten males of Bar Mitzvah age or older are needed for extended, and therefore more meritorious, public prayer in Orthodox synagogs.

Mishnah—Rabbinical work in six sections, containing development of the laws of the Torah; codified by Judah Ha-Nasi, about 200 C.E.

Mitzvah (pl. *Mitzvot*)—Commandments. According to the Talmud there are 613 *mitzvot* in the Torah which each Jew should obey. A number of lists have been made by sages as to what the exact 613 are. The compendium of Maimonides has been accepted as standard. However, even the most Orthodox Jew cannot live by them all. Many require living in Israel; some are connected with agriculture in a society of observant Jews; many deal with the Temple and its sacrificial cult. The others deal with every aspect of life. And Jewish law has added many more requirements to the original sum.

The word *mitzvah* has taken on additional meaning, so that it often connotes a good deed as well.

Mizrach—The East. A plaque bearing the word *Mizrach* in Hebrew, sometimes worked in artistic fashion, placed on the east wall of the synagog or the living room of Orthodox Jews, so that worshipers will know which way to face when they pray.

Mohar—The bridal purchase price in olden days, paid by the groom to the bride's father.

Mohel—A ritual circumciser.

Motzi—The blessing over the bread, thus the traditional grace before meals.

Musaf—Additional prayers in traditional synagogs on the Sabbath and festivals. On these days additional sacrifices were offered in the Temple in Jerusalem. These prayers take their place. They are recited after the Torah reading of the *Shacharit* service.

Nadan—Dowry.

Natan—A gift to the bride from the groom and his family, which took the place of the *mohar*.

Ner Tamid—Eternal light. Every synagog has a *ner tamid* above the ark.

Neshamah Yeterah—According to tradition, an additional soul, granted to the observant Jew so that he might be able to enjoy the spiritual joy of the Sabbath to the utmost.

Oneg Shabbat—The delight of the Sabbath. A reception and collation held by Orthodox Jews on Sabbath afternoons, and by Reform Jews after Sabbath eve worship.

Oreach—A guest. It always has been a *mitzvah* to bring home a guest for a Sabbath or festival meal.

Peot—Corners. Originally these were the corners of the field which the farmer was not allowed to harvest, for the crop there belonged to the poor. Later it came to mean the male's sidelocks, which are never cut by the Orthodox.

Pesidige—*Kosher* for Passover use.

Pidyon ha-Ben—Redemption of the son. A ceremony held on the 30th day of the first-born son in which he is redeemed from the priests.

Pikuach Nefesh—The preservation of life. This has always been a cardinal rule of Judaism. Even the most Orthodox Jew may break every law but three to preserve life. These three are adultery, worship of idols, and murder.

Piyut (pl. *Piyutim*)—Special liturgical poetry written especially for the High Holy Days, by medieval poets, often in elaborate verse. The most prolific poet was Rabbi Eleazar Hakallir of ninth-century Palestine.

Pizmon—The central hymn of the penitential *Selichot* prayers.

Prosbul—A legal device instituted by Hillel that made it possible to borrow money in the period just before the sabbatical year, when all debts would be cancelled.

Rosh Chodesh—The first day of the new month.

Sandek—A position of honor at a ritual circumcision. The man who holds the child during the operation.

Sargenes—See *Kittel*.

Seder—The order of the service and meal at the home ceremony on the first (and second) evenings of Passover.

Selichot—Penitential prayers for the Days of Awe and the preceding period.

Sephardim—Descendants of the Jews of Spain and Portugal. The language of modern Israel is Sephardic Hebrew. (See note on *Ashkenazim.*)

Seudah Shelishit—The third meal of the Sabbath. To satisfy the Talmud's requirement for three meals on the Sabbath, a brief meal in the synagog in the afternoon.

Sevivon—The Hebrew name for *dreidel,* a spinning top.

Shaddai—The Almighty.

Shadchan—Marriage arranger.

Shacharit—Traditional morning prayers. Originally at dawn.

Shalach manot—The sending of gifts, usually baked goods, at Purim.

Shamash—Synagog sexton; *shammis* in Yiddish. Also, the attendant candle on Chanukah *menorah.*

Shechinah—The indwelling presence of God. When men do deeds of goodness, when they discuss the teachings of the Torah, when they live lives of holiness, the *Shechinah* is near.

Shechitah—Ritual slaughter.

Shehecheyanu—Blessing recited at happy occasions and at festivals. "Who has kept us in life, sustained us and brought us to this time."

Sheitel—Wig. Orthodox wives keep their heads covered at all times except in complete privacy. Some achieve this by wearing a kerchief over their heads; many by wearing a *sheitel.*

Shekia—The time to light Sabbath or holiday candles, usually twenty minutes before sundown. The time of course varies with the passing of the year and from latitude to latitude.

Sheloshim—The thirty-day period of mourning, not as restrictive as the *shivah* period.

Shemitah—The sabbatical year, occurring every seventh year. The land lay fallow, slaves went free, and all debts were cancelled.

Sheva Berachot—Seven benedictions, recited as part of the wedding ceremony. They express our thanks to God for the blessings of marriage and look forward to the reign of peace and joy for all.

Shin—The first letter of the word *Shaddai,* the Almighty, which appears on the outside of a *mezuzah* or *tefilin* box and is visible on the parchment within a *mezuzah.*

Shiur—A study session, especially of the Talmud and its commentaries.

Shivah—The seven days of mourning following the burial of a close relative. From the Hebrew for seven, *sheva.*

Shochet—Ritual slaughterer. He must pass a stiff examination in Jewish law, animal anatomy, and in personal observance before he is allowed to practice.

Shtetl—The small village of Poland, Lithuania and Russia in which the Jews had been forced to live by the ukase of Catherine of Russia. It became the symbol of economic degradation and yet spiritual attainment.

Shul—The Orthodox synagog. From German word for "school."

Shulehof—The synagog courtyard.

Shulchan Aruch—The "Prepared Table," compendium of Jewish law and practices, codified by Joseph Karo of Safed in the sixteenth century.

Shul Klopper—In the days before alarm clocks, a man who went from house to house and banged on the shutters to waken people for early services.

Simchah (pl. *Simchot*)—An occasion of rejoicing.

Siyum—The festive meal that marks the completion of the study of a tractate of the Talmud.

Sukah (pl. *Sukot*)—Temporary shelter hung with greens, for holiday of Sukot.

Taam (pl. *Teamim*)—Musical symbols of the *trop,* printed with the vowels, above or below the text, in Hebrew Bibles.

Tachrichim—Burial clothing. Consists of shroud and undergarments of white linen.

Taharat ha-Mishpachah—Family purity. Regulations concerning the connubial relations of husband and wife.

Takanah—Rabbinic emendation of talmudic law.

Talit—Prayer shawl worn by traditional Jews.

Talit Katan—Small *talit.* See *arba kanfot.*

Talmud—Vast compendium of Jewish wisdom, mainly development of law of Mishnah. There are two versions of the Talmud: The Babylonian, the more important, finished about 600 C.E.; the Palestinian or Jerusalem, finished about 500 C.E. Both are mainly legal in character and mostly in Aramaic.

Techinah (pl. *Techinot*)—Penitential prayers and supplicatory poems.

Tefilin—Phylacteries.

Tenaim—Engagement conditions for marriage.

Tevilah—Immersion in the *mikveh*. Apart from ritual purification, the Jews have always regarded physical cleanliness as important because, as Hillel taught, the human body reflects the divine image of God.

Trop—Ancient musical forms by which the Bible is chanted at traditional services.

Tsaar Baale Chayim—Causing sorrow to any living creature. Cruelty to any animal was always strictly prohibited, so that slaughter was as painless as possible, and hunting for sport frowned upon as a *chukat goyim,* a despised custom of the non-Jews.

Tzitzit—The fringes of the *talit*.

Tzom Esther—The fast of Esther. A fast ordained for the day before Purim, to commemorate Esther's fasting.

Unterfirers—Family friends who play a special role in the traditional wedding procession.

Ushpizin—Hospitality in the *sukah*. The host invites poor and other guests to join in his meal, after first inviting Abraham, Isaac and Jacob and the past spiritual dignitaries of early Israel.

Vidui—Confession. There are two kinds of *vidui:*

  (1) At Yom Kippur services, the long confession of sins.

  (2) Traditional death-bed confession. "When a man is sick and near to death, let him make confession" (*Shabbat* 32a).

> *O my God and God of my fathers! Let my prayer come before Thee, and disregard not my supplication. Oh, forgive all the sins I have committed from my birth until this day. I am abashed and ashamed of my evil deeds and transgressions. Pray accept my pain and suffering as an expiation, and forgive me my wrongdoing.*
>
> *Father of the orphan and Judge of the widow, protect my beloved kindred, with whose souls my soul is bound up.*
>
> *Into Thy hand I commit my spirit; Thou hast redeemed me, O Lord God of truth.*

Hear, O Israel: The Lord, our God, the Lord is one.
The Lord He is God. (ABRIDGED)

Yarmulka—Skullcap.

Yatom—Orphan.

Yeshivah Bachur—A student at a *yeshivah* or talmudical academy.

Yichus—Pedigree, especially an ancestry of rabbis and scholars.

Yizkor—The initial word of the prescribed prayer of the *Hazkarat Neshamot,* the Memorial Service. The word *yizkor* (may He remember) has become the title of this service for most people.

Yomim Noraim—The Days of Awe. The ten-day period beginning with Rosh Hashanah and ending with the close of the Day of Atonement.

Yovel—Jubilee. After seven times of the Sabbatical year, forty-nine years, came the *yovel,* the Jubilee year.

Zeman Matan Torah—The Time of the Giving of the Torah, Shavuot.

Zemirot—Table songs for the Sabbath.

Zohar—Mystical work, source-book of the Kabalah, written in Aramaic in the form of a commentary on the Torah, probably by Moses deLeon of Spain in the thirteenth century. The Zohar's intent is to point out the mystical bases of the Torah.

Appendix

Prohibited Marriages

TABLE* OF PROHIBITED DEGREES OF CONSANGUINITY AND AFFINITY

Biblical Prohibitions   *Talmudical Extensions*

A. CONSANGUINITY

a. In the Ascending Line

1. Mother; Grandmother (paternal as well as maternal).

b. In the Descending Line

2. Daughter (implied in granddaughter).
3. Granddaughter (son's or daughter's daughter); Son's or daughter's granddaughter.

c. Collateral Consanguinity

4. Sister and half-sister (either born in wedlock or not).
5. Father's sister; Grandfather's sister.
6. Mother's sister; Grandmother's sister.

B. AFFINITY

a. Through One's Own Marriage

7. Wife's mother; Wife's grandmother; Wife's stepmother not strictly prohibited, but objectionable.
8. Wife's daughter (stepdaughter).

* Moses Mielziner, *The Jewish Law of Marriage and Divorce,* p. 41.

205

The harvest of the soil, of mind, of spirit

9. Wife's granddaughter.

10. Wife's sister (during the lifetime of the divorced wife).

b. Through Marriage of Near Blood Relation

11. Father's wife (stepmother); Father's or mother's stepmother.

12. Father's brother's wife; Mother's brother's wife; Father's uterine brother's wife.

13. Son's wife; Grandson's or great-grandson's wife.

14. Brother's wife (except in the case of levirate).

Bibliography

BOOKS ON REFORM JUDAISM

COHON, SAMUEL S.: *Judaism,* Union of American Hebrew Congregations, Cincinnati, 1948.

DOPPELT, FREDERICK A., AND POLISH, DAVID: *A Guide for Reform Jews,* Bloch, New York, 1956.

FELDMAN, ABRAHAM J.: *Reform Judaism,* Behrman House, New York, 1956.

FREEHOF, SOLOMON B.: *In the House of the Lord,* Union of American Hebrew Congregations, New York, 1951.

————: *Reform Jewish Practice,* Volumes I and II, Hebrew Union College, Cincinnati, 1944 and 1952.

————: *Reform Responsa,* Hebrew Union College, Cincinnati, 1960.

————: *Recent Reform Responsa,* Hebrew Union College, Cincinnati, 1963.

PLAUT, W. GUNTHER: *The Rise of Reform Judaism,* World Union for Progressive Judaism, New York, 1963.

————: *The Growth of Reform Judaism,* World Union for Progressive Judaism, New York, 1965.

Rabbi's Manual, Central Conference of American Rabbis, New York, 1961.

SCHAUSS, HAYYIM: *The Jewish Festivals,* Union of American Hebrew Congregations, Cincinnati, 1938.

————: *The Lifetime of a Jew,* Union of American Hebrew Congregations, Cincinnati, 1950.

SCHWARTZMAN, SYLVAN D.: *Reform Judaism in the Making,* Union of American Hebrew Congregations, New York, 1955.

207

SCHWARTZ, JACOB D.: *Responsa of the Central Conference of American Rabbis,* Union of American Hebrew Congregations, New York, 1954.

Union Home Prayer Book, Central Conference of American Rabbis, New York, 1951.

OTHER BOOKS CONSULTED

ARIEL, SH'LOMO ZALMAN: *Encyclopedia Meir Netiv,* Masada, Tel Aviv, 1964.

BIRNBAUM, PHILIP: *A Book of Jewish Concepts,* Hebrew Publishing Company, New York, 1964.

EISENSTEIN, J. D.: *Otzar Dinim U'minhagim,* Hebrew Publishing Company, New York, 1917.

GLUSTROM, SIMON: *The Language of Judaism,* Jonathan David, New York, 1966.

GOLDIN, HYMAN E.: *HaMadrikh,* Hebrew Publishing Company, New York, 1939.

Guide to Jewish Ritual, Reconstructionist Press, New York, 1962.

The Jewish Encyclopedia, 12 volumes, Funk and Wagnalls, New York, 1901.

MONTEFIORE, C. G., AND LOEWE, H.: *A Rabbinic Anthology,* Jewish Publication Society, Philadelphia, 1960.

NEWMAN, LOUIS I., AND SPITZ, SAMUEL: *The Talmudic Anthology,* Behrman House, New York, 1945.

VAINSTEIN, YAACOV: *Cycle of the Jewish Year,* World Zionist Organization, Jerusalem, 5721 (1961).

THE JEWISH CHRONICLE HOLIDAY SERIES

JACOBS, LOUIS: *Rosh HaShanah,* London, 1959.
————: *Yom Kippur,* London, 1951.
FABRICANT, ISAAC N.: *Succoth,* London, 1958.
LEHRMAN, S. M.: *Hanukkah and Purim,* London, 1958.
PEARL, CHAIM: *Shavuoth,* London, 1959.
————: *The Minor Festivals,* London, 1963.
GOLDMAN, SOLOMON: *The Sabbath,* London, 1961.